kids'
places to play

By Jeanne Huber and the Editors of Sunset Books, Menlo Park, California

SUNSET BOOKS

VICE PRESIDENT AND GENERAL MANAGER: Richard A. Smeby
VICE PRESIDENT AND EDITORIAL DIRECTOR: Bob Doyle
PRODUCTION DIRECTOR: Lory Day
OPERATIONS DIRECTOR: Rosann Sutherland
RETAIL SALES DEVELOPMENT MANAGER: Linda Barker
EXECUTIVE EDITOR: Bridget Biscotti Bradley
ART DIRECTOR: Vasken Guiragossian

STAFF FOR THIS BOOK:

MANAGING EDITOR: Bridget Biscotti Bradley
WRITER AND PROJECT DESIGNER: Jeanne Huber
ART DIRECTOR: Vasken Guiragossian
PHOTO STYLIST AND PROJECT BUILDER: Ryan Fortini
ILLUSTRATOR: Melanie Powell, Studio in the Woods
TECHNICAL CONSULTANT: Jay Beckwith
COPYEDITOR: Carol Whiteley
PAGE PRODUCTION: Janie Farn
PREPRESS COORDINATOR: Danielle Javier
PROOFREADER: Peggy Gannon
INDEXER: Nanette Cardon

Cover photograph by Chuck Kuhn. Treehouse built by the TreeHouse Workshop. See pages 76-85 for more information.

10 9 8 7 6 5 4 3 2
First printing January 2004
Copyright ©2004
Sunset Publishing Corporation,
Menlo Park, CA 94025.

Library of Congress Catalog Card Number: 2003109533
ISBN 0-376-01059-2
Printed in the United States

For additional copies of *Kids' Places to Play* or any other Sunset book, call 1-800-526-5111 or visit us at www.sunset.com.

CONTENTS

places to play

ASK ADULTS WHAT THEY REMEMBER OF childhood and chances are their eyes will light up as they tell you about the places they played: the sandbox where they built canals and sand castles, the playhouse where they served pretend tea, the garden where they caught frogs or turned hollyhock flowers into fairy dresses. Today's kids need these magical experiences, too. But many children spend most of their playtime indoors, and when they do go out it's often to heavily supervised day-care centers and schoolyards. The children may have little chance to build and tear down and build again, or to concoct elaborate fantasy adventures, or to simply sit and stare at a spider spinning a web. Yet these are the very experiences kids need if they are to develop their sense of creativity, competence, adventure, and wonder. A well-designed home play setting can give children these opportunities. This chapter explores the elements of successful play spaces and shows how to integrate them with the rest of a family garden. You'll also find tips on planning play spaces with help from the best experts you can get: the kids who will use them.

planning for play

Planning a successful home play environment isn't just a matter of scaling back what's found on public playgrounds. The never-ending options seem fresh because the park is big, the kids don't go there every day, and there are plenty of other kids. But move the same equipment into a backyard, have it available day after day, remove the other children, and guess what? Even the most elaborate play structure soon grows stale.

To maintain children's long-term interest, home play spaces need to encourage open-ended activities that won't grow old because the kids have a way to keep changing them. A sandbox, for example, can be a kitchen for sand pies one day and a castle for knights and ladies the next. And forts and tree houses can serve both as splendid "away" spaces where kids can read and sketch and as club-houses when friends come over.

In public playgrounds, safety rules dictate everything. In a home play setting, parents can adjust the opportunities to match their comfort level and the skill and judgment of their children. Play equipment still needs to be designed to minimize the chance of injury, of course, but some of the rules that hold for public playgrounds can be relaxed. For example, in public spaces, swings may not be combined with other play structures because there's too much chance of a child running across the path of another child swinging. But in a backyard, where far fewer children may be playing at once, combination play structures often work best because kids incorporate all the features into their fantasy play. Plus, free-standing swings take up far more space than most families can spare.

In planning a play space, remember that the adult's job is to provide the stage, not to write the script. A fully furnished, fully equipped playhouse may not be as satisfying from a child's point of view as one in which there are still curtains to be made and walls to be painted and decorated—so encourage kids to help with these finishing touches.

Children have different needs at different ages, and the whole sweep from infancy to teen years passes in a flash. Keep this in mind as you design play spaces. The best structures are either convertible to other uses or they are small or simple to disassemble, making them easy to pass on to another family.

GETTING KIDS INVOLVED IN PLANNING

Building a play space should be a joyous process that involves the children as much as possible. But if you ask them what they want, they may think only of the swing sets and slides that they've seen. Unlock fresh ideas by sketching or building models together and talking about how the kids will play there. The models needn't show construction details—that's for an adult to figure out—but they can illustrate basic shapes and fun details. For decorating ideas, look at picture books in which the characters have clever houses or forts.

A father and daughter constructed this model of a climbing structure to communicate their basic design to a builder, using popsicle sticks and balsa.

Although children's play preferences change as they age, one activity holds its appeal: swinging. Two swings are better than one; conversations happen there.

This garden pond, about 4 by 8 feet, was once a fine sandbox for toddlers. But as the kids grew, they needed a larger canvas. To convert the old play space into a garden pond, the family added four courses of stone, a plastic liner, a circulating pump, and water.

Use a child's construction kit, such as a set of Legos, to show possibilities, or build with small pieces of pine, balsa, or other wood. Hobby stores usually sell suitable pieces by the bag as well as by the piece. The stiffer woods need to be cut with a small, fine-tooth saw, also sold at hobby shops. Thin balsa cuts easily with kids' scissors, but thicker pieces require a utility knife. Even many first-graders can use utility knives safely, provided an adult watches to make sure all cuts are made by pressing down into the balsa as it rests on a cutting board. To hold pieces together, use thick craft glue, which grabs fast and doesn't require clamps. For non-wood elements, improvise with items around the house. A piece of cardboard can double as a slide. A jar lid and string can work for a tire swing. For fold-down projects, pieces of tape can simulate hinges.

WHAT KIDS ENJOY IN OUTDOOR PLAY SPACES

1–2 YEARS

- Safe spaces to walk or run
- Steps to climb and descend
- Blocks to stack and topple
- Sand and water with containers to fill and dump
- Wagons to load and pull
- Swings with seats that kids can't fall from
- Short slides, with an adult assist (2+)
- Tunnels to crawl through
- Simple, cozy playhouses
- Child-size tables and chairs

3–5 YEARS

Many of the above, plus:
- Props that encourage role-playing
- Suitable surfaces for riding tricycles
- Climbing nets
- Ladders and climbing structures
- Stationary balance beams
- More challenging slides
- Swings with seats that allow kids to pump themselves

6–9 YEARS

Most of the above that relate to sand, water, swings, and playhouses, plus:
- Even more props for role-playing
- Building materials
- Garden crafts materials
- Tire swings that twirl
- Forts
- Suspended balance beams
- Taller climbing structures
- More challenging slides, including banister slides
- Climbing walls
- Garden spaces to plant and harvest
- Pets that can go outdoors

10–13 YEARS

Most of the above, plus:
- More elaborate forts and tree houses, especially those they help build
- Trolley rides
- More challenging climbing structures and climbing walls
- Ball courts and flat, open lawns for games
- Gardens of their own

family gardens

Backyard play areas don't need to look like they've been airlifted in from an institutional playground. Artful placement and clever design create spaces the entire family can use.

INTEGRATING PLAY AREAS INTO A LANDSCAPE

When Andrea and Brian Mackin began landscaping their rural property, they installed two features specifically for their children: a small sandbox and a rather large swing set. Then Brian, a potter, built a shop near the house, and the family embarked on a much more ambitious plan to landscape and fix drainage problems. A construction crew brought in a dumptruck load of sand, which sat for a week. Every day the kids came home from school, tore off their good clothes, and ran for the sand pile. The parents got the message: The kids needed a larger sandbox.

Learning from their first sandbox, the family located the new one in clear view of the kitchen window. Now the kids feel independent but not abandoned, and the parents appreciate being able to go about their activities while the kids are playing. The parents can also see out to other play areas, including a shallow artificial stream with a bridge and a big, flat lawn area where neighborhood kids gather for volleyball, soccer, baseball, and impromptu chasing games.

Top left: It wouldn't work in all areas, but in this Northwest garden the generously sized fire pit is one of the features adults and kids love most. Top right: Ian floats boats and concocts elaborate scenarios involving trolls passing over and under the bridge across the family's artificial stream. Although a child could conceivably trip and drown in the water, the parents figure that the risk is no greater than other dangers people face—and survive—every day. As a result, their kids enjoy a play space that's endlessly fascinating.
Bottom left: Through the Dutch door on their playhouse, Katie and Ian can chat with their dad. Set in an island of perennials and towering Douglas firs, the playhouse is just secluded enough to give kids a sense of being off in their own private space.
Bottom right: When kids play in sand and water, the mess almost inevitably gets tracked into the house. But under the outdoor shower, Katie rinses off before going in.

Kids from a whole neighborhood fit in the sandbox, which measures about 14 by 14 feet. Peeled cedar logs, cut on the property, provide a rim.

For safety, swing sets require a wide ring of shock-absorbing mulch all around, which can leave the play equipment marooned on an island of cushioning. This yard, however, connects play space and garden seamlessly because the family spread a thick layer of pea gravel both in the swing area and on adjoining paths.

DRAWING KIDS INTO THE GARDEN

The two children of Denise and Bryan Johnson have a tree house, a rope swing, a sandbox, and a trolley ride, but two garden features that aren't always thought of as play spaces often prove a stronger magnet. One is a "fairy garden." The other is the family's mini-farm, populated by a few chickens and ducks, a goat, and a heifer.

In the fairy garden, everything from the plant selection to the paving carries out the theme. The parents add to the magic by sprinkling in a little fairy dust as needed to ensure that unseen visitors whisk away gifts that the children put out.

And yet, the garden avoids being too precious. The children helped plant, so some parts aren't arranged as perfectly as a garden designer might specify. The kids are also free to pluck flowers and alpine strawberries, and they bring toys into the garden and incorporate the setting into their fantasy play. "The reason it's such a good place for kids is that it's not perfect," Denise says. "The kids run through it and use it."

Above: In the fairy garden, holiday lights threaded into arbors twinkle year-round. *Far left:* Parents and kids worked together to decorate the mortar that holds stone steps in place. The family embedded bits of jewelry, toys, and improvised art, including a spark plug fashioned into a dragonfly. *Middle left:* A watering can never runs empty thanks to a small recirculating pump plumbed into a basin below. Strings of beads create the look of a sparkling waterfall. *Left:* Garret balances himself on a big knot as he swings over a gentle slope along the edge of the lawn.

PLANTING A FAIRY GARDEN

PLANT AND ITS PLAY POSSIBILITIES

Bleeding heart, *Dicentra spectabilis*
Turn the flower upside down and pull the little petals back to see the head and arms of a fairy.

Lady's-mantle, *Alchemilla mollis*
Downy leaves cause water droplets from dew or rain to bead up, giving fairies a place to wash their faces.

Lamb's ears, *Stachys byzantina*
The soft, fuzzy leaves make fairy towels. Leaves also work well as skirts for flower dolls.

Mouse plant, *Arisarum proboscideum*
Peek under the heart-shaped leaves of this shade lover to see a flowering structure that looks like the long tail of a mouse scampering down a hole.

Oriental poppy, *Papaver orientale*
Use dried seedpods as heads for fairy dolls. Either cut the pods with a stem long enough for the body, or leave the pods standing and dress in place to create fairies that hover in the garden.

Hardy fuchsia, *F. types*
Pull off buds and pop between fingers. Or let flowers open and pretend they're fairy earrings.

Balloon flower, *Platycodon grandiflorum*
Pull off buds, which look like blue balloons, and pop.

Gunnera, *G. manicata*
The monster leaves (up to 6 feet wide) make kids feel as small as fairies.

11

A SMALL CITY YARD THAT GROWS WITH A CHILD

It's one thing to offer multiple play opportunities in a large yard. It's harder to pull that off in a small space. This backyard, just 30 by 30 feet, packs in a sandbox, a kid-friendly water feature, a tricycle-riding path, a theater, a vegetable plot, and a raspberry patch. Perhaps best of all, the newly planted landscaping was designed so that it would grow to give Joseph, 3, and Malia, 1, plenty of places to hide and build forts.

Designed by Patricia Strehlow, a Seattle landscaper, the garden also meets the needs of the parents, Rick LaFrance and Lisa Cardus, and the family dog. Lisa sits in the theater to rock and nurse Malia while Joseph digs in the sandbox. Because Joseph is a few steps down, he feels off on his own, yet there's nothing scary because Mom is within eyesight. When the family entertains, the open-sided theater becomes a serving area.

The family paved the circular pathway with gravel, which is firm enough to work as a tricycle raceway for Joseph. They planted the raised bed alongside the yard with lettuce, sweet-smelling herbs, and two kinds of child-size tomatoes

(Yellow Pear and Sweet 100). Strawberries edge the vegetable path and will eventually cascade down the side of the bed. The raised bed, which doubles as a retaining wall, is too high for Joseph to reach, so the family incorporated a turtle stepping stool into the garden design.

Left: The theater is open to fresh air and has a roof. Some days, the family uses it for art projects too messy to do in the house. This day, Malia and her mom are preparing to curl up with pillows where there's no risk of mud.

Above: With its yin-yang design, the 12-foot circle at the center of the garden provides space for sand play and enough lawn to experience the joy of bare feet. The sand is nearly 2 feet deep, guaranteeing that Joseph can "dig to China" if he wants.

Right: Made by an artist partly out of recycled oxygen tanks, the water feature doubles as garden art and a safe play spot. Joseph collects dribbles for use in the sandbox and makes music by banging on the bells. He also enjoys climbing up and down the stone ledge.

Far right: A welcoming gate signals to kids that this garden is for them. The design was cut from a single sheet of paper by artist Sharyn Sowell and sandwiched between sheets of Plexiglas®.

A WONDERLAND FOR ACTIVE KIDS

With five boys aged 6 to 22, Candace and Erik Jagel needed plenty of outdoor play spaces.

They were also busy remodeling their century-old farmhouse. So as parts of their yard were ripped into for remodeling projects, they put in features that appeal to youngsters of a wide range of ages.

Their first big project was a basketball court, installed in the final stages of redoing a well and well house. A contact made in that project led to a builder who added a tree house. The family's oldest boy spent many happy hours outfitting it with a drawbridge, wooden bunks, and screened-in windows. Earth-moving needed for a new septic system provided the impetus for a big sandbox (see page 32).

Supported by three trees and a post, the tree house is set next to a sharp drop-off so the entry is almost at ground level but the view out the back is high up in branches.

KIDS AND ANIMALS

Perhaps because they have minds of their own, animals greatly enrich children's play experiences. The more outdoor interaction they offer, the better, which is why some families keep a few backyard hens.

Little kids delight in hunting down snails for the hens to crunch, and laugh in glee when the chickens eat bits of weeds offered as treats through the coop's wire netting. And, of course, there are always the eggs. Sean, 7, fills his shirt with multicolored ones to sell at a local farmers' market.

SPORTS COURTS

Although her boys wanted a basketball court, Candace Jagel worried that a big expanse of concrete might look ugly and barren. She now says it's one of the best things the family has added.

The court measures about 22 by 23 feet, slightly smaller than a half-size regulation court.

Because it's big, open, flat, and dry, the court is often where the family heads whenever they have a project that needs to be done in a big space. The older boys built bike ramps and spent days practicing their soaring skills there. Candace assembled walls for a turkey barn on the court. The younger boys use it to draw elaborate designs with chalk.

Lucas, 9, and his brother Sean practice shots with their dad on the family's basketball court.

And, of course, the kids play basketball. The backboard, made of acrylic, hangs from a 4-by-4 steel pole. Although it looks slim and sleek, a pole such as this is a real heavyweight. The manufacturer recommends setting the pole into a wide hole (2 feet across and 2 feet deep) and filling the hole and the hollow pole with dry concrete mix to add rigidity and to eliminate condensation, which leads to rust. These two steps together take about 900 pounds of concrete mix—before water is added.

A flat, paved pad serves many purposes in a yard. Sean draws large pictures with chalk while Lucas races in circles on his scooter.

building with kids

It sounds great to involve kids in building their own play spaces, but the reality is that it's often a frustrating experience for kids and adults alike. Pace projects so that when kids are there to help, there's something useful for them to do.

Unfortunately, the first stages often go slower than everyone expects, which can get things off on a sour note. Try having the kids help clear the site and stake it out, then go off to do something else while the adults fine-tune the foundation. When the actual building commences, get the kids involved again.

Children are often eager to cut wood and pound nails, two jobs that seem the essence of building. But to make headway with a handsaw requires both a sharp saw and a way to hold the wood steady. Young children need to clamp the wood to a work surface, which should be a little lower than waist height. (If the workbench is higher, have a stepstool handy.) Tell very young children

to saw with both hands on the handle, even though a professional would never do it this way. They'll make faster progress, won't tire as easily, and can't cut themselves.

Older kids should saw the standard way, gripping the tool with one hand. If clamps aren't handy, they can use their body to hold the wood down, just as professional carpenters often do. Place the wood on a slightly elevated surface, such as a milk crate or a deck step, and have the child hold the work in place with the knee or foot opposite the sawing arm.

GREAT JOBS FOR KIDS

3–5 YEARS
- Help design
- Hold tape measure
- Hand nails or tools
- Fetch things
- Shovel sand or pea gravel
- Paint
- Help decorate
- Help clean up

6–7 YEARS
All of the above, plus:
- Drill (with adult help)
- Tighten screws in pre-drilled holes
- Tighten bolts
- Sort parts
- Note and check measurements
- Help check for square angles
- Remove nails on salvaged lumber

8–11 YEARS
All of the above, plus:
- Nail, especially downward
- Mix concrete, but only one sack at a time
- Cut boards to length where angle isn't critical
- Power saw with jigsaw if wood is clamped and an adult is watching

12 YEARS AND OLDER
Depending on the kid, pretty much anything, including:
- More complex saw cuts
- More independent drilling (have the kids pre-drill all screw holes; it's hard for them to put enough pressure on a drill to get self-drilling screws to seat properly)

SCRAPES, SLIVERS, AND WORSE

Scrapes and slivers aren't the worst accidents that can happen, but they sure can ruin a kid's day. Construction details that lessen the chance of these injuries make perfect projects to farm out to kids.

Rounding over sharp edges on wood might seem like a job best done with a router. On a kid-oriented work site, however, it may make more sense to do it by hand with a rasp. Even young children can work safely and surprisingly fast.

Older kids enjoy using a power drill to prepare joints so that they won't have protruding bolts or nuts, which can cause nasty cuts. To allow use of bolts whose length matches the thickness of the wood being fastened, oversize holes, called counterbores, need to be drilled on the back of the wood. Young children can't keep a drill straight and steady enough for the wide bit that's needed for the counterbore, but middle school–age kids usually can.

For general job-site safety, make sure there are plenty of adult helpers in proportion to the number of kids involved. One adult can supervise two children, but if the ratio is higher and the kids are young, they often wind up waiting for advice on how to proceed. While they wait, accidents can happen.

RASP
Direct the rasp down and slightly forward to keep long splinters from forming.

MASKING TAPE

DRILL
Bolted connections call for carriage bolts, which have rounded heads. So sharp bolt ends don't protrude on the back, drill a recess for the nut before you drill the bolt hole. Use a spade bit that makes a hole wide enough for a socket wrench and add masking tape as a depth stop, set to the thickness of the nut and washer. The center point guides a twist bit ($\frac{1}{16}$ inch wider than the bolt) the rest of the way through. A scrap block underneath keeps the exit hole from tearing.

KIDS AND HAMMERS

A few tips lead to more success when children want to pound nails. First, have them, not you, hold the nail, and tell them to keep their eyes on it as they hammer. There's something about hand-eye coordination that keeps people from smashing their own fingers when it's done this way. Kids should give the nail a few taps to set it, then move their hand away and drive the nail home with harder blows.

Coach children to position themselves so they can swing the hammer in an arc to one side of their body. When kids hammer in front of their belly, the nail usually bends.

If kids instinctively grip midway on the handle, let them, especially if they're young or the hammer is heavy. They'll gain in control what they sacrifice in force. The easiest kind of nailing is straight down. Good tasks for kids include nailing floorboards and assembling parts that can be laid out on a flat surface. If kids don't have the strength to drive nails, try helping them to use a drill and screws instead.

good tools for children

TOOL BELT Useful for keeping nails and screws close at hand. It's not essential, but kids like the look.

SCREWDRIVER A 4-in-1 screwdriver offers small and large bits in two styles: Phillips and straight.

SMALL HAMMER Find one under 12 ounces from a manufacturer that also makes hammers pros use. These hammers have properly domed faces to help nails go in straight.

WRENCHES Adjustable wrenches are handy, but fixed-opening wrenches aren't as likely to slip or damage bolt and nut heads. When there are many bolts to tighten, kids appreciate a socket set with a ratchet.

HANDSAW Efficient sawing means using most of the blade on each cut, so the blade must not be too long for kids. A toolbox saw has a blade about 15 inches long. A pistol-grip saw with a 12-inch blade allows young children to hold with both hands.

BIT AND BRACE This old-fashioned hand tool gives children the power they need to drill large holes. It can also be fitted with screwdriver bits to produce plenty of torque.

CLAMPS For kids, it's just as it is with adults: You can never have too many.

TAPE MEASURE Contractors' tapes with 1-inch blades are too heavy and bulky to fit in a kid-size tool belt. A half-inch tape with a blade no more than 12 feet long is more suitable.

JIGSAW Because there's no chance of kickback and the blade is always within clear view, this is a power saw suitable for older kids to use (with supervision). Makes curved or straight cuts.

RASP AND SANDING BLOCK Shape wood with a rasp, which cuts fast, or a Microplane rasp, which also doesn't clog. Smooth wood with sandpaper or a foam-type sanding block; blocks are easiest for children to use.

EAR PROTECTORS Kids are especially sensitive to the noise of power tools and enjoy wearing ear protectors. Adult-size earmuffs usually adjust to fit.

CORDLESS DRILL A 12-volt version makes a wonderful "first power tool" for older children to use. Because there's no cord, it's safer outdoors than a corded drill.

PAD AND PAINTBRUSH Inexpensive brushes work best for small projects because they can be washed easily. For big expanses, avoid spatters by using paint pads instead of rollers.

BUCKET Buckets carry tools, sand, and dirt. Avoid 5-gallon buckets, whose dimensions present a drowning hazard to toddlers.

GLOVES If you can't find kid-size work gloves, look for gardeners' stretch gloves.

GOGGLES Eye protection is a must whenever power tools are used.

choosing materials

Kids don't need to be using tools every minute to feel part of the action. Often, it's enough to just watch and hear about the various steps.

Time, skill, and money become crucial factors when families build play spaces. Have enough of all three and projects can be as lavish as you wish. If only two are adequate, something needs to give. But building to suit the family's needs—now and in the future—is also key.

Settling on the right material for a project involves an assessment of how long it is likely to engage a child's interest. A simple climbing structure that challenges a 2-year-old, for example, doesn't have to be built to meet cabinet-makers' standards or involve use of rot-resistant wood. But a jungle gym intended to serve several siblings' needs into middle-school years requires a different approach.

Climbing structures that will be left out in the weather for years require construction details that won't develop into safety problems. Parts in contact with the ground must resist rot and insect attack. Above-ground pieces need to be sturdy enough, and connections must not rattle

loose. As a general rule, use posts that are at least 4 by 4 inches, and use horizontal supports for platforms that are at least 2 by 6 inches. Railings need horizontal pieces that are at least 2 by 4 inches and balusters that are at least 2 by 2 inches.

When a playhouse or fort is built to last, key concerns include a suitable foundation and a roof that sheds water. Attend to these and the rest of the structure will generally do fine, even if every joint isn't perfectly cut. Generous roof overhangs not only look good, they go a long way toward keeping the rest of the structure dry and thus safe from rot and termites. If the building will eventually be converted to another use, such as a potting shed or an art studio, it needs a doorway that adults can get through and enough headroom inside to stand up straight. Placing the door on a peaked end and leaving the interior rafters exposed keeps the overall building from becoming too massive.

ROT-RESISTANT WOOD

Now that wood infused with an arsenic-based preservative is being phased out for residential use, other types of rot-resistant lumber are becoming more available. Several new kinds of pressure-treated lumber are on sale now, and more are being developed. Options also include naturally durable woods, plastic lumber, and plastic-wood composites.

For play structures, the natural alternatives, such as cedar and redwood, may be especially appealing. Be aware, however, that the second-growth cedar and redwood on sale today are not as durable as old-growth lumber was. If you choose these species, select pieces with the darkest color for places where rot resistance matters most—such as parts in contact with soil. Any whitish sections of cedar or redwood are no more rot resistant than ordinary pine.

Plastic lumber and composite lumber are suitable for decking on play structures, but most types

PROTECTING WOOD FROM THE SUN

Wood that occasionally gets wet but quickly dries usually doesn't rot. Its major enemy is more likely to be the sun's ultraviolet light, which breaks down lignin, the "glue" that holds wood fibers together. Over time, UV rays can leave wood looking dry and feeling rough and splintery. Stains and paints prevent this damage because their pigments block UV rays. Stains generally are easier to keep up because they don't peel. They are definitely the best choice for horizontal surfaces out in the weather, where paint can trap moisture within the wood, leading to decay.

RED CEDAR CA-B REDWOOD ACQ JUNIPER

don't have the stiffness needed for posts, joists, deck rails, and other critical areas. The materials are free of splinters and generally require little or no maintenance, both big assets. But they can be heavy, which may require beefing up the support structure. And some types, especially in dark colors, absorb so much heat that they can be unpleasant to play on when the sun's out. Test a sample before you build.

If you opt for preservative-treated wood, be sure to ask the supplier which type of fasteners to use. Many of the preservatives contain copper, which in wet conditions can cause a battery-like reaction that strips zinc off galvanized fasteners, allowing them to rust. With electrogalvanized screws and nails, which look shiny and smooth, the zinc disappears quickly. Even the thicker, dull-gray coating on hot-dipped galvanized fasteners may not last long with some types of pressure-treated lumber. You may need stainless steel, especially in locations where failure of the fastener would be a safety hazard.

In all types of pressure-treated lumber, the protection extends only to the shell of the wood. Builders must paint cut ends with a preservative, such as copper naphthenate. Otherwise, insects and the fungi that cause rot can simply tunnel into the wood through the exposed untreated fibers. Below are some options for rot-resistant lumber.

CA-B: A type of pressure-treated lumber also known as copper azole because of its preservatives. Azole is a fungicide registered for use on food crops. The B signifies the specific formula. Use hot-dipped galvanized fasteners or those with ceramic coatings.

ACQ: A type of pressure-treated lumber. The letters stand for "alkaline copper quaternary." The lumber contains copper and a chloride that together corrode galvanized coatings. Use stainless-steel fasteners where safety or appearance matters.

REDWOOD: An old standby that today comes from second-growth stands. Hot-dipped galvanized fasteners are fine, although tannins in the wood can react with iron in the coating and cause dark stains. With stainless-steel fasteners, you won't see stains.

RED CEDAR: Similar to redwood but less splintery. Also contains tannins, so choose fasteners as you do for redwood. Aluminum fasteners also work well with redwood and cedar but aren't widely available except as nails.

JUNIPER: Available in some parts of the West. Very rot resistant but knotty. Quite flexible when newly cut, so horizontal supports built of juniper should be beefier than usual.

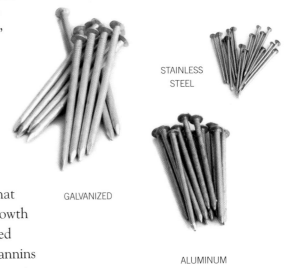

STAINLESS STEEL

GALVANIZED

ALUMINUM

making projects "kid size"

Proper sizing is a key factor in designing play equipment. Sometimes the issues pertain purely to fun. For example, young children love cozy playhouses, as small as 3 by 3 feet. That's about the space available in a hut fashioned from a refrigerator box. But older kids may want enough room to spread out a few sleeping bags, each of which measures 33 by 75 inches in full size. With walking space between them and a bit of scrunching at the toes, that probably means a fort of at least 6 by 6 feet.

Often, sizing affects safety. One of the cardinal rules for play equipment designers is to allow no openings that are between 3½ and 9 inches wide, because these spaces can trap and strangle a child. The smaller dimension is the narrowest torso width of small 2-year-olds, while the larger measurement equals the widest head diameter (measured from the chin to the back of the head) of big 5-year-olds.

In public playgrounds, designers usually separate 2- to 5-year-olds from 5- to 12-year-olds because there is no way to size equipment so that it works for everyone. Safety standards are set to accommodate either the smallest children or the tallest in each age group, depending on the safety issues. This translates into play equipment dimensions that aren't always necessary in home settings. Step height, for example, is usually set at no more than 9 inches for young children because that is the maximum for the tiniest children in the 2- to 3½-year-old age group. The tallest children in the same group, however, can handle steps 18 inches apart—the same distance as small 12-year-olds.

Top: A playhouse sized only for young children makes a cozy hideaway.
Bottom: A playhouse with more generous dimensions and an adult-sized door can be turned into a potting shed when the kids outgrow it.

WHAT "KID SIZE" MEANS AT DIFFERENT AGES

AGE GROUP	DOORWAY HEIGHT	GUARDRAIL HEIGHT*	RUNG SPACING**	CHIN BAR HEIGHT***	MINIMUM SEAT WIDTH
2–3½ yrs.	32–43 inches	22–24 inches	9–18 inches	38–49 inches	6–9 inches
5½–6½ yrs.	38–51 inches	22–29 inches	14–27 inches	46–62 inches	7–11 inches
11½–12½ yrs.	52–69 inches	30–39 inches	18–31 inches	62–84 inches	9–16 inches

*to prevent tipping
**on horizontal ladders, "monkey bars"
***where feet bottom out

GETTING UP AND DOWN

On play equipment, staircases, ladders, and ramps become play elements in themselves. But they still need to serve the practical purpose of getting kids up and down safely.

When designing these features, there are two key factors to consider. First, the general rule to never allow any openings that are larger than 3½ inches and smaller than 9 inches applies here. Even if your kids are past the age when you need to worry about them squeezing through a 3½-inch opening, there's no point building something that may endanger another child some day. If a staircase needs steps between those measurements that could trap a child, close off the opening between the treads.

Also be careful to space rungs or treads uniformly. People can easily adjust to varied step heights when they scramble over rocks or climb trees. But when climbing a staircase or ladder, even young children subconsciously gauge the distance between the first couple of steps and are likely to stumble if following steps aren't spaced exactly the same.

ROPE LADDER
Attach top and bottom for easier climbing.

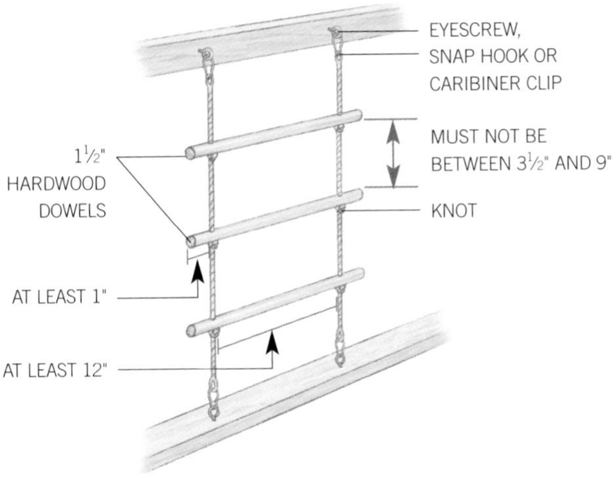

EYESCREW, SNAP HOOK OR CARIBINER CLIP

1½" HARDWOOD DOWELS

MUST NOT BE BETWEEN 3½" AND 9"

KNOT

AT LEAST 1"

AT LEAST 12"

LADDERS
Best angle is 75° from the ground. Support treads with wood, not just nails or screws.

TREAD SUPPORT

INSET INTO GROOVE

75°

AT LEAST 9"

12" TO 20" WIDE

RAMP

LIP RESTS ON RUNG

HALF-ROUND MOLDING

15°

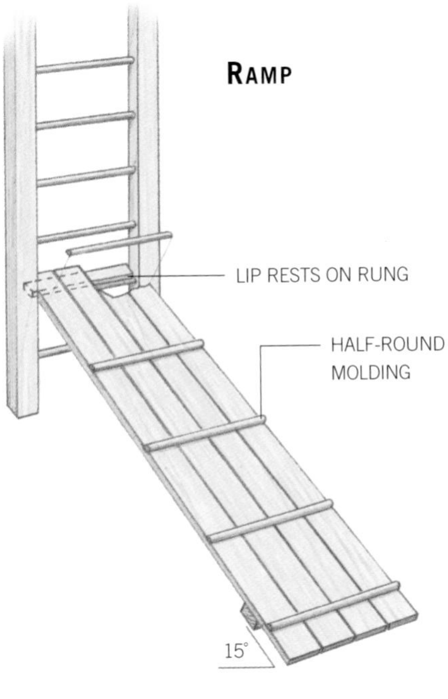

RUNG LADDER

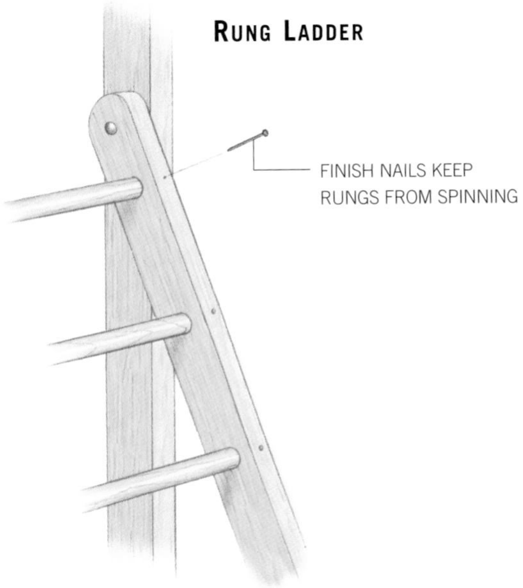

FINISH NAILS KEEP RUNGS FROM SPINNING

sand and water *NO ONE NEEDS TO TELL A CHILD*

how to play in a sandbox. Kids just know. They also know that if you add water to sand, it's more fun. Bring in a few props, such as plastic animals or toy trucks, and children are off on one adventure after another. This chapter explores ways to build sand and water features that please both children and adults. Kids don't really care how the sand and water are made available to them. A pile of sand straight out of a dumptruck and a hose filled with water work just great. It's the adults who need sand and water features to be more carefully designed so that they fit into the landscape, minimize dirt tracked into the house, and avoid safety hazards. Proper placement resolves many issues. In this chapter, you'll see how clever design and smart material choices—such as water faucets that shut off automatically—lead to sand and water features that keep everyone in the family smiling.

sand and water go together

Child-development experts put sand and water right up there with blocks and dress-up clothes as essential play elements that every child has a need—even a right—to experience. The reason: They allow children to create worlds of their own imagination.

Kids love to feel the squish of sand between their toes. They like to dig, scoop, and let the grains fall. If a water source is nearby, children make damp sand, which holds together enough to be molded or sculpted.

Water also holds special appeal in its own right. Kids are fascinated by the interplay of light on water, by things that float on it, by drips and splashes. Just as with adults, children often consider a water feature one of the most popular components of a garden.

Careful placement of sandboxes and water features is important, both to minimize mess and to promote healthy play. Unlike mud, which clings stubbornly to shoes

and clothes, sand drops off as soon as it dries. Locating a sandbox and water feature some distance from the house can make a big difference. So can separating the sandbox from paved patios (where sand will need to be swept up) with surfacing on which sand can fall and remain. A gravel path or a lawn makes a good transition.

When considering placement, think about the direction and angle of the sun. A water feature may look best in sunshine. Sand-boxes need some shade or children won't be able to play there much of the day.

A total absence of sunshine in the sandbox isn't a good idea, however. Ultraviolet rays from the sun, a powerful disinfectant, need to reach the sand to help keep it sweet smelling and sanitary. The best compromise may be a setup that allows morning sun and afternoon shade, particularly in the summer.

WHAT MAKES A GREAT SANDBOX?

Bigger's better when it comes to sandboxes. Except in the smallest yards, sandboxes should be at least as big as a sheet of plywood— 4 by 8 feet. The sand needs to be deep so kids won't hit dirt when they dig. The minimum depth is 12 inches. Double that amount is much better.

Sandboxes need some type of rim to contain the sand. This can be an earth berm, wood, stone, or concrete. Don't enclose the bottom of the box, however. Water needs to drain.

Provide a flat space that can serve as a baking surface for sand pies or a launching pad for toy helicopters. Locating this within the sandbox, rather than along an edge, helps keep sand inside. If you do opt for a flat rim, try to place any overhang on the outside; if it must be on the inside, check often for spiders, which love dark spaces. If you build a ledge, make it strong enough to support an adult who can't stoop to join children in their play.

Top left: Adding rocks is an easy way to adapt a garden water feature so that it's safe for all but the youngest of crawlers. *Below*: A flat space of some type is as crucial in a sandbox as a countertop is in a kitchen.

SELECTING SAND

The best play sand consists of clean, rounded grains all approximately the same small size. Sand with these qualities builds fine castles when damp and doesn't leave kids muddy.

Damp sand stays together because of the adhesive force of water molecules that fill spaces between the grains. When the grit is irregular or large, grains fall apart.

Rounded grains, found on beaches and in some underground deposits, work better than sharp-edged sand, which comes from quarries where rock is blasted apart. Rounded grains never pack tight when dry. Grains of sharp-edged sand interlock, becoming difficult to dig.

There is no official standard for sandbox sand, so one supplier's "play sand" may be quite different from that of another. If you have several options, look at them to see which has the finest, most even grit. Moisten a handful and clinch it. If the shape holds, this sand will make good castles. If technical data is available, select sand with a grain size between 30 and 50 and a silt and clay content below 5 percent.

ALL-PURPOSE
SAND

PLAY SAND

SILICA-FREE
SAND

Buying sand by the truckload is far less expensive than buying it by the bag, but to get it delivered you may need to buy several cubic yards. By the bag, however, it's easier to handle.

For a magical sandbox, consider colored sand. Manufacturers coat the grains with a plastic polymer that locks in the color. Once dry, it doesn't wash off.

SAFE SAND Read the fine print on a bag of play sand and you may be shocked to see a warning that inhaling the dust may cause cancer. It's there because extremely fine shards of crystalline silica, which comprises approximately 70 to 90 percent of typical sand, have been linked to serious lung disease and cancer among construction workers exposed to large amounts day after day.

The U.S. Consumer Product Safety Commission, which regulates safety issues involving children, has not evaluated whether

COLORED SAND

crystalline silica in play sand is hazardous to children. Their exposure to it is likely to be far less than construction workers'.

But to minimize risk, you can:

- Have children play with damp sand, which generates no dust.
- Buy play sand, which tends to have grains approximately the same size, rather than all-purpose sand, which has a mixture that includes particles small enough to be dangerous.
- Consider buying sand free of crystalline silica. One non-silica play sand contains mostly feldspar, a mineral not known to be hazardous (see Resource Guide).

DEALING WITH CATS

To keep cats out of sandboxes, use plastic mesh, not solid covers. Solid covers don't allow sunshine to reach the sand, and they create good conditions for spiders. Look in the garden department for plastic netting sold to deter deer or birds. It comes in pieces big enough to cover even the largest sandbox. To hold the mesh in place, slip it over cup holders (a type of metal hook) screwed to the outside of the sandbox. Be sure to point the curved end down.

kid-safe water features

An old millstone rigged to a recirculating pump that bubbles water up out of a hole in the middle gives even young children safe access to water. Kids can splash, collect drips in a cup, or even sit in the slight depression where water collects. Antique millstones are hard to find, but new ones can be purchased (see Resource Guide).

A child can fall and drown in just a few inches of water, but with clever design, water features don't have to be dangerous. Water can trickle out of a fountain onto smooth rocks, for example. Or it can flow through a narrow channel in which a child's head won't fit.

The most hazardous situation is a pool or pond with steep sides. Ponds with sloping sides and shallow depths near the edges are far less dangerous. Never create water features using 5-gallon buckets or anything with similar dimensions. Toddlers, whose center of gravity is slightly higher than the bucket's, can easily tip over and drown in one in even a few inches of water. Once children tip over, the bucket's narrow width doesn't let them get upright.

It's also important when planning a water area not to create a slick surface where children may slip. Parents should consider the neighborhood situation as well as the age and judgment of their own children when they decide how rigid or relaxed to be about giving children access to water features where a child could conceivably drown. When children are old enough not to be foolish, the edge of a pond is a magical place to play.

NO-WASTE WATER

Besides safety, there is another issue to consider when children will have access to water: They often forget to turn it off. If you install a self-closing faucet, the water will flow only when a hand is on the tap. A self-metering faucet is another option. It dispenses a specific amount of water and then shuts off. You may need to shop at a specialty plumbing-supply company or on the Internet for either of these faucet types (see Resource Guide).

Automatic water bowls designed for pets or farm animals can also be used. They connect to a hose and include a valve that opens only as needed to keep the bowl filled. Bowls for farm animals may be the best option because they typically are designed to be bolted in place.

Water fountains intended as garden art can often be adapted to make them safe for children simply by adding mesh or stone to block access to the container where water collects. To boost the play value of a recirculating fountain, install a float valve (also available at farm stores) to automatically replace water that's carried off to a sandbox or other play space.

FLOAT VALVE

SELF-METERING FAUCET

boat sandbox

Kids can sail away to countless adventures in this clever sandbox, which includes a hidden base that allows sand to be twice as deep as the boat is high. The sail provides shade. And the seats serve as platforms for baking sandbox cookies.

In most construction projects, builders begin with the foundation and then build the structure on top. For this project, it makes more sense to work in the opposite order. First, build the boat; next, the foundation. Then, excavate and move the pieces into place.

The boat shown here was built out of redwood. Building the sandbox is almost as easy as assembling a simple box, except for a few special cuts. To give the sandbox its boat shape, the side pieces need to be cut at a 45-degree angle. That requires beveling the edges of the end pieces at a 45-degree angle so the shelves can sit flat. No special joinery is required; screws or bolts hold everything together. If you wish, add a bell and a steering wheel, and prepare to wave as children sail off to magical lands.

SEWING THE SAIL

The sail was made from a polyester fabric manufactured to upholster outdoor furniture. Acrylic fabric sold for this purpose will also work well. However, some outdoor fabric comes only in relatively narrow widths. If you choose this type, splice pieces together to get one sail large enough to span the width of the sandbox. Cut 36-inch-wide fabric into pieces 12 and 6 feet long, then cut the short piece in half lengthwise. Sew the short lengths end to end and join to the long piece. Hem the edges and ends, using a double overlap of about ¼ inch on the sides and 2 inches on the ends. Insert a large grommet at each corner, following the instructions on the package.

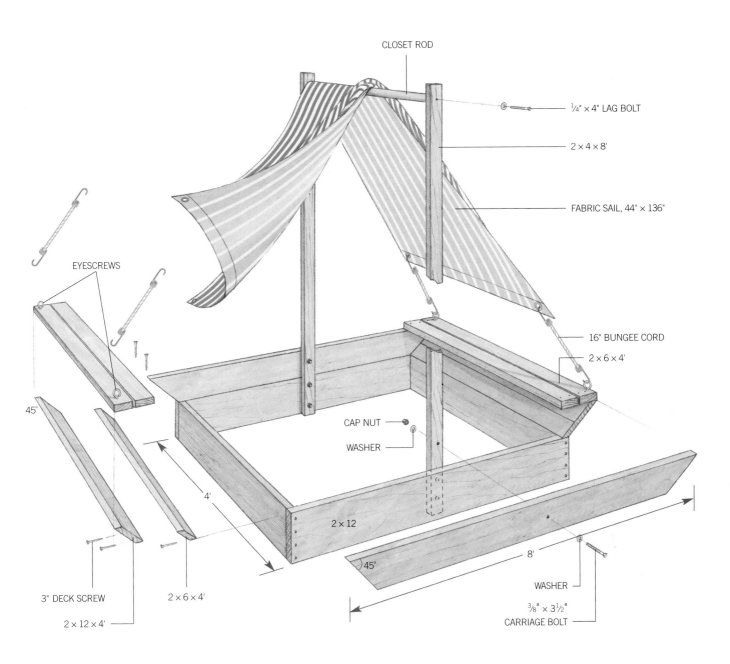

CLOSET ROD

¼" × 4" LAG BOLT

2 × 4 × 8'

FABRIC SAIL, 44" × 136"

EYESCREWS

16" BUNGEE CORD

2 × 6 × 4'

45°

CAP NUT

WASHER

4'

2 × 12

8'

3" DECK SCREW

2 × 6 × 4'

45°

WASHER

2 × 12 × 4'

⅜" × 3½"
CARRIAGE BOLT

MATERIALS

- Six 2 × 12 × 8' planks rot-resistant wood
- Three 2 × 6 × 8' planks rot-resistant wood
- One 2 × 4 × 8' piece rot-resistant wood
- Closet rod, 1¼" × 4'
- Two ¼" × 4" lag bolts
- Two ¼" cut washers
- Four ½" × 1½" eyescrews
- Four 16" bungee cords

- Six ⅜" × 3½" carriage bolts
  with 12 washers and 6 cap nuts
- Box of 3" galvanized deck screws
- Four yards 45"-wide outdoor fabric
  (or 6 yards 36"-wide fabric)
- Roll of thread
- Four large grommets
- Two cubic yards sand

BUILDING INSTRUCTIONS

1 Because the sandbox sides are cut at a 45-degree angle, the top and bottom edges of the end pieces must be beveled at the same angle. Use a table saw, a jigsaw, a hand plane, or, as shown here, a circular saw. Adjust the saw's guide to a 45-degree angle before making the cut.

2 Assemble the boat upside down on a flat surface so that the top edges align. With deck screws, attach the end pieces to the sides. Fill the gap on each end with a 2 by 6, beveled to match the other end pieces.

3 Using the upside-down boat as a guide, mark the 2 by 12s that will become the boat's foundation. The side pieces should equal the length of the boat at its base. Cut the side pieces to fit. The foundation requires only straight cuts.

4 Mark the sandbox perimeter with spray paint. Then dig out an area slightly larger than the exterior of the box. The depth should equal the width of a 2 by 12—about 11 ½ inches.

5 With a helper, move the foundation box into the hole and check the sides to make sure they are level. Shim with small rocks if necessary. Then set the boat on top. Add a few angled deck screws to tack the pieces together.

6 Prepare the masts while they are flat on the ground. In each 2 by 4, drill a $\frac{1}{4}$-inch hole $1\frac{1}{2}$ inches down from the top. At the other end, drill three $\frac{3}{8}$-inch holes. Locate them 4, $15\frac{1}{2}$, and 19 inches from the bottom.

7 After raising the masts and screwing them in to the boat frame so they are plumb, cut the closet rod to fit the distance between the tops of the masts. Clamp a scrap of wood to one mast while you secure the other end with a lag bolt.

8 Add the benches to the base with deck screws, spacing the boards about $\frac{1}{2}$ inch apart. Then insert one screw eye at each corner. For added torque, use the shaft of a screwdriver.

9 Fill the boat with sand, stopping about 4 inches from the top. This boat took about 2 cubic yards of sand.

10 Spread the sail over the closet rod and attach to the eyebolts with bungee cords. If there's too much slack, adjust the tension by knotting the cords.

a sandbox built for building

When Candace and Erik Jagel tore into their yard for a basement waterproofing system and a new septic field, their boys wasted no time discovering the play value of a sand pile trucked in by the construction crew. So as the yard went back together, the family included an oversize sandbox in their landscaping.

With heavy equipment already on hand to do the hard work, the family sculpted the slope in front of the house to create a nest for a circular sandbox 12 feet in diameter. Because the digging was effortless, they made the sand a generous 3 feet deep. The sand is set directly into the earth, and a rim of masonry blocks defines the perimeter. Sandbox accessories include leftover drainpipe, which the boys use as a chute to carry things down the hill.

The family shares a well with several neighbors. Fearing that the boys might overtax the supply, the parents at first had a rule against using a hose in the sandbox. The lure of water with sand proved irresistible, however. An underground water line equipped with a self-closing shower valve solved the problem. Now the boys pull a chain or lower a handle and water gushes out—but only as long as they hold the tap open.

THE EASY WAY TO INSTALL A KID-FRIENDLY WATER SOURCE

Extending permanent outdoor plumbing can be a big project if it requires digging a trench several feet deep. A far easier method is to bury a hose a few inches deep. If you use a type lined with foam (see Resource Guide), it won't burst from freezing water. The foam compresses to accommodate the expansion as ice forms.

Connect the hose to a faucet that keeps the water from being siphoned back into the drinking-water supply if pressure drops. Outdoor faucets installed within the past decade should have this health-protection feature. Older faucets can be retrofitted by adding a fitting called a backflow preventer. Note that most modern outdoor faucets drain to eliminate the danger of ice, but not if hoses are connected. Unscrew the sandbox water line as winter approaches.

Right: There is no trench to dig in this easy method for extending a water line. Align a flat spade next to the hose and slice straight down into the soil about 4 to 6 inches. Rock the spade back and forth to create an opening in which the hose will fit. Soil that's too compacted needs to be loosened first with a few quick jabs of a pick. Without removing the spade, stuff the hose as deep as possible into the opening. Then push the dirt back into place and move on to the next section.

Far right: Sean, 7, fills a bucket easily from a self-closing valve designed primarily for showers. The chain, intended to enable short people to reach the handle, wound up being the favorite way to turn on water for Sean and his brother Lucas, 9.

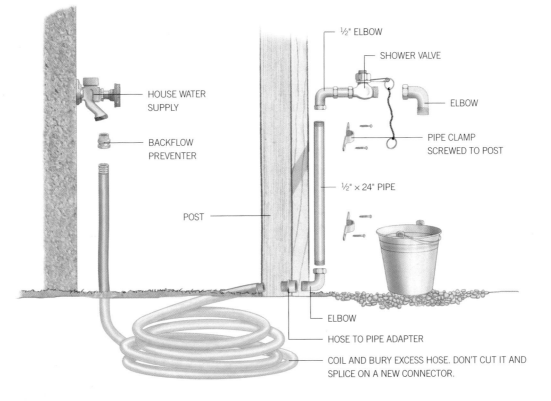

HOUSE WATER SUPPLY

BACKFLOW PREVENTER

POST

½" ELBOW

SHOWER VALVE

ELBOW

PIPE CLAMP SCREWED TO POST

½" × 24" PIPE

ELBOW

HOSE TO PIPE ADAPTER

COIL AND BURY EXCESS HOSE. DON'T CUT IT AND SPLICE ON A NEW CONNECTOR.

MATERIALS

- Foam-lined hose of sufficient length
- Backflow preventer, if needed
- Rot-resistant post, 4' or 5' long
- Gravel or concrete mix to fill hole around post
- Two ½" pipe clamps, with screws
- Hose-to-pipe adapter
- Teflon™ tape (wrap pipe threads before assembly)

- Three ½" 90-degree galvanized pipe elbows, each with one internal and one external thread
- Threaded galvanized pipe, ½" × 24" long
- Self-closing shower valve*
- Grate, gravel, or bark to protect faucet area from becoming muddy
- * Available from plumbing-supply stores

an inventor's sandbox

Give kids sand and water, add wheels, inclined planes, and other simple machines, and there's no end to the magical things they may learn. As in artist Rube Goldberg's creations, the point isn't how much sand they move but how intricately they do it.

This sandbox features a play board with numerous attachment points. The board rises 3 feet across the back of the sandbox, allowing enough room for devices to be arranged in a way that one action triggers another and then another. The inclined planes, for example, can be set up to channel sand into the wheel, which in turn will dump sand into the box with the trapdoor. These various configurations keep Bryan, 2½, and his friends busy for hours.

Borrowing a concept long used on climbing walls, including the wall shown on page 104, the board features a network of T nuts inserted from the back. The play board devices bolt into these nuts. To protect against bolts coming loose, use those that are long enough to thread through the T nuts and project far enough beyond to hold a lock washer and a standard nut. Snug these up against the T nuts when you fasten things to the play board. Where very young children play,

parents should tighten the bolts because washers are too small to be safe for them to handle.

For older kids, omit the extra nut and lock washer and provide a wrench so that they can loosen and move the parts themselves. Designing and adding new features is half the fun.

The sandbox itself is easy and quick to build. It consists of four layers of 4-by-4-inch posts topped by a rim of 2-by-6-inch wood. This construction allows sand about 12 inches deep with a few extra inches to minimize spills. Because this sandbox is located next to a pine tree, it was not possible to dig out soil beneath the box. On other sites, excavating would allow deeper sand or shorter walls.

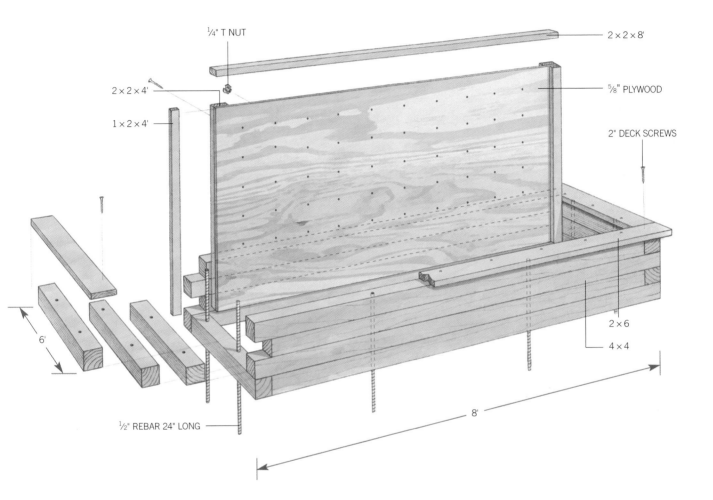

1/4" T NUT

2 × 2 × 8'

2 × 2 × 4'

5/8" PLYWOOD

1 × 2 × 4'

2" DECK SCREWS

6'

2 × 6

4 × 4

1/2" REBAR 24" LONG

8'

MATERIALS

- Posts: eight pieces 4 × 4 × 8', four pieces 4 × 4 × 12'
- Planks: two pieces 2 × 6 × 6', one piece 2 × 6 × 8'
- Back supports: one piece 2 × 4 × 8' (cut in half)
- Trim: one piece 1 × 2 × 8', one piece 2 × 2 × 8'
- Rebar: eight pieces 1/2" × 24"
- * Use rot-resistant wood

- One box 2" deck screws
- One 4 × 8' piece 5/8" exterior plywood
- Forty 1/4" T nuts
- Forty-eight cubic feet sand
  (approximately 1 3/4 cubic yards)

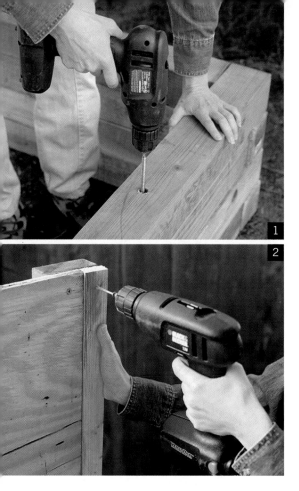

OUTFITTING THE PLAY BOARD

Equip the play board with ready-made items as well as devices you build at home. When interest in one piece of equipment wanes, replace it with something fresh. Encourage kids to dream up their own gear.

A. This funnel, sold for changing car oil, comes with tubing attached. An alternative would be a standard funnel, a length of tube, and a hose clamp or piece of duct tape to hold the parts together.

B. Two plastic cups suspended from a pole that pivots create an adjustable scale. To keep each cup upright, an eyebolt extends through a hole in the bottom. A nut and washer on each side of the plastic hold the bolt in place. Instead of a single pivot point there are several holes, so kids can test the effect of having the arm longer on one side than the other.

C. Two plastic soda bottles taped together provide a see-through double funnel when the ends of both bottles are removed. If you use the same concept but leave the end on one bottle, the contraption becomes an hourglass. Suggest that kids use it to time how long it takes to build a castle a foot high.

D. A simple box made of 1-by-4-inch pine provides hours of fun thanks to the trapdoor at the bottom. Pivoting on a hinge, the door stays shut thanks to a magnetic cabinet latch. But when kids pour enough sand into the box, the weight overwhelms the magnet and the door pops open, sending the sand cascading out.

E. A simple shelf gives kids a handy place to store sand toys, plastic teacups, or decorations for sand art projects. Building the shelf is very easy. Just take a length of 1-by-3-inch pine and nail, screw, or glue it to a piece of 1-by-1-inch pine. Drill $5/16$-inch holes into the 1-by-1 for the mounting bolts and the shelf is ready to install. Paint before mounting if desired.

F. Reminiscent of the Chutes & Ladders board game, these simple inclined planes channel sand down the board. Kids can also tie a cup and a toy car to opposite ends of a short string and see how much sand needs to be poured into the cup to pull the vehicle uphill. The ramps are lengths of 1-inch corner molding.

Below the ramps is a red sand spinner. Modeled after a water wheel, it has four compartments made of two rectangles of 1-by-3-inch pine cut to interlock. The wheel is $1/4$-inch plywood in a $6^1/2$-inch-diameter circle. The mounting bolt fits into a $3/16$-inch hole drilled through the center. Washers on both ends allow the wheel to spin freely. As sand pours in, the wheel begins to rotate and eventually spills its load.

BUILDING INSTRUCTIONS

1 After stacking the 4-by-4 posts so their ends overlap in opposite directions, use an extra-long bit to drill two $1/2$-inch holes through all layers of each side. Then pound rebar through the holes until the metal is flush with the top of the wood. A 2-by-6-inch rim, screwed onto the side and front 4 by 4s, hides the exposed rebar tips.

2 Follow the instructions for installing T nuts on page 106, then screw the plywood to 2-by-4-inch supports at both ends of the sandbox. Leave a $1^1/2$-inch gap on both sides for 1-by-2-inch trim pieces. A trim piece across the top covers the remaining exposed edge of the plywood.

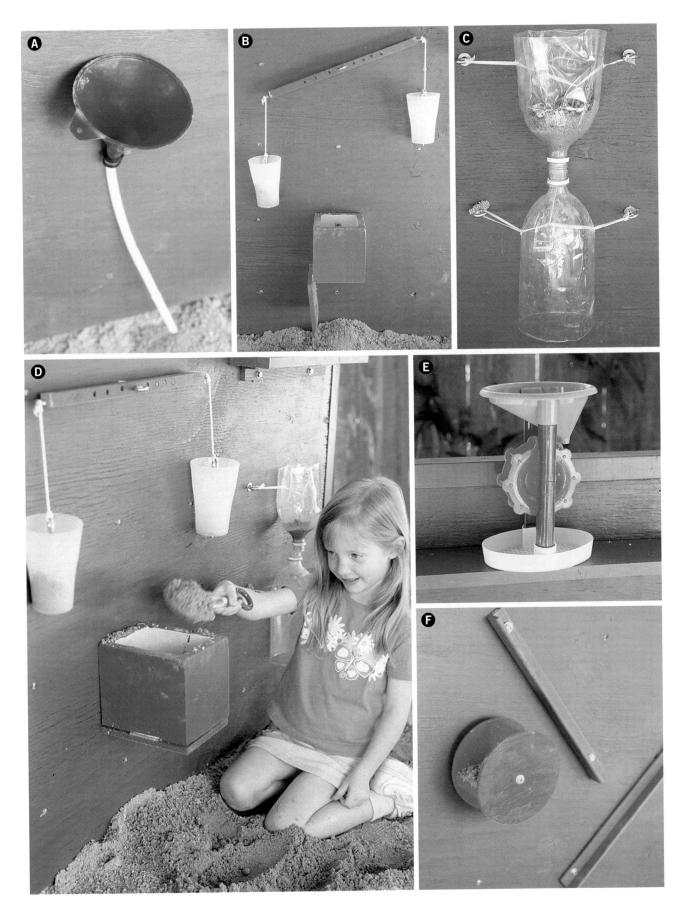

dual-purpose garden art

A garden water feature can serve both as a decorative element and as a kid-friendly water source, as this fountain shows.

The simple setup consists of a fountain that sends water cascading into a buried basin. To protect a child from falling in, the basin is topped by the stiff wire mesh of an attic louver. A grate or other type of permeable cover also works, provided it is attached securely and can support the weight of any person who might stand on it. A layer of rocks hides the louver.

Access to an outdoor electrical receptacle that is properly grounded and protected with a GFCI (ground fault circuit interrupter) breaker is required. A small recirculating pump, which sits in the basin, pushes the water back up to the fountain through a short piece of clear plastic tubing. This is piped through the wall that supports the fountain so that the tube is out of sight.

You can buy a fountain and a recirculating pump as part of a set or purchase them individually. Check the label to make sure the pump is capable of lifting the water as high as you want, and be sure to buy tubing that's the diameter listed on the pump's package.

This wall fountain allows Rachel, 5, to play with dribbles or collect them in a cup. But if too much water is taken out, the fountain will soon run dry. To avoid having to refill the basin frequently, add a float valve. Sold at farm-supply stores for keeping stock watering troughs full, a float valve can be connected to a hose so that water is automatically refilled when it drops below a certain level (see page 27).

BUILDING INSTRUCTIONS

Dig a hole big enough for the basin and excavate the perimeter so that the louver will sit flush with the top of the soil. Place the basin in the hole and level the rim. Connect the tubing to the pump and, if desired, thread it through two holes in the wall so that water enters the fountain from the back. You can also hide tubing running up the front of the wall with plants or lattice. The tubing should be cut at a length that allows the pump to sit solidly on the floor of the basin. To ensure this, connect the fountain, then extend the tubing to the bottom of the basin, allow a little slack, then cut. The power cord attached to the pump should be pulled out of the basin toward a GFCI outlet. Fill the basin almost to the top with water, and plug in the pump to make sure that the stream of water coming from the wall fountain hits the basin. Adjust the pump as necessary. Once the pump level is set, mark where the fountain pump's cord and tubing cross the basin's edge and cut a notch. Then place the louver on top of the basin, making sure that the lid extends beyond the basin walls and that it is slightly below ground level, allowing the rock cover to be smooth with the surface (see illustration). Cut a piece of wire mesh or screen and lay it over the louver. Spread small to medium-sized stones over the mesh, blending the edges into the surrounding landscape. Have an adult stand on the stones to make sure it is stable, and then plug in the pump again to start the fountain.

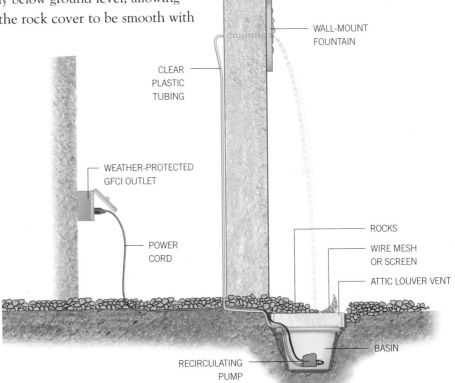

SUPPORT WALL

WALL-MOUNT FOUNTAIN

CLEAR PLASTIC TUBING

WEATHER-PROTECTED GFCI OUTLET

POWER CORD

ROCKS

WIRE MESH OR SCREEN

ATTIC LOUVER VENT

BASIN

RECIRCULATING PUMP

MATERIALS

- Recirculating pump
- Wall-mount fountain
- Length of clear plastic tubing (diameter depends on pump requirement)
- Plastic basin approximately 14" × 14"
- Attic louver vent approximately 19" × 15"
- Piece of wire mesh or screen, approximately 2' × 2'
- Rocks to cover screen

rain-gutter regatta

A few lengths of plastic gutter, four corner pieces, and six leveling devices create this fun boat-racing course.

Modeled after a setup often used by Scout groups, which stage regattas on straight lengths of gutters set out on sawhorses, this project uses a circular route made easy with corner pieces.

With a little ingenuity, the idea can also be easily turned into a semi-permanent garden feature similar to the miniature outdoor railroads some families use as landscape accents.

Adults involved in this project sketched out various ways to build the supports, but the three teenagers involved, Kaza, Chris, and Matt, came up with an even simpler method. They screwed scraps of ¾-inch-thick wood, about 4 by 4 inches, to the ends of 1-by-2 wood stakes. Screwing into end grain usually doesn't

make for long-lasting joinery, but on this project it worked just fine.

The teenagers assembled the course first, discovering that it takes quite a bit of force to slip and snap gutter sections into the corner fittings and to take them apart again. With practice, however, the work became easier.

When the course was complete, the teens set out the supports so that one would be under each corner and at midpoint on the long spans. They hammered the supports into the ground until the tops looked about level, then filled the gutter with water and were happy to discover that it did not leak. The setup was now ready for the younger kids—Sophia, Graham, and Jacob—to huff and puff to make their boat go fastest.

Top: *Chris cuts the gutter-end pieces with a hacksaw. Clamping pieces of wood underneath stabilizes the plastic so it's easier to cut.*

Bottom: *Kaza connects a length of gutter to a corner piece, which includes a rubber gasket that creates a watertight seal. Meanwhile, Matt taps a support post into place. The kids discovered that hammering straight down is important. Sideways blows can split the wood on the top of the support piece.*

MATERIALS

- Three 10' pieces plastic gutter
- Four gutter corner pieces
- Six wooden pads, approximately ¾ × 4 × 4"

- Six 1 × 2 × 18" wooden stakes
- Six drywall screws
- Toy boats

41

DINOSAUR DIG

Many scientists believe that dinosaurs didn't become extinct; they evolved into birds. Stare at a chicken's feet some day and you're likely to see the connection.

In a sandbox, evolution can go backward. Bury chicken bones in the sand and let the kids dig them up and piece them together as a dinosaur. To prepare, boil the bones (before or after eating the meat) for about 1½ hours and allow them to cool. Pick the bones clean, using a plastic scrub pad or old toothbrush on stubborn bits of gristle. If you want them white, put them out in the sun or bleach them. When the bones are dry, they're ready to hide. Count them before you bury them so you'll know when the hunt is over. Non-meat eaters can substitute plastic bones.

Even kindergarten-age children can arrange the bones to make a fairly respectable dinosaur. Passionate junior paleontologists can go on to make intricate models of specific types.

SAND KITCHEN

Like adults who cook, sandbox chefs try out new recipes when presented with kitchen gadgets they haven't had before. Shop thrift stores and garage sales for items that stir, sift, and mold. Among the possibilities:

- Funnels
- Ice cream scoops
- Small nylon brushes
- Measuring cups
- Spatulas
- Pastry tins
- Squirt bottles
- Rolling pins

To decorate sand cakes and cookies, kids can gather leaves or flowers from the garden. As a special treat, fill a shaker jar with colored sand (see page 26) for a sandbox version of candy sprinkles.

OUTDOOR BLACKBOARD

With chalk and a place to use it, a child can be amused for hours. There are two ways to make outdoor chalkboards (besides improvising with flat, relatively smooth surfaces such as sidewalks).

TRUE SLATE CHALKBOARD As old schools are torn down or converted, their blackboards often wind up in salvage stores. Cut pieces to a manageable size with a diamond blade in a circular saw. Be sure to wear a respirator rated for filtering fine particles, such as a disposable with double elastic bands. Filters labeled "dust masks" aren't good enough. Slate countertop material, available at companies that deal in stone, is another option. So are roofing slates (new or salvaged), though they have a slightly rougher surface. Standard sizes for roofing slates go up to 24 by 16 inches.

For any outdoor chalkboard, provide a waterproof storage container for the chalk.

PAINTED CHALKBOARD Blackboard paint converts a variety of smooth materials into chalkboards.

For an outdoor board, use a large patio paver, sanded exterior-grade plywood, or a specialty plywood known as MDO, for "medium-density overlaid." (Don't confuse MDO with MDF, a particleboard-type product that is for interior use only.) MDO has a very smooth phenolic resin overlay on one or both surfaces. Coat all sides of any wood-based panel with an exterior wood primer before applying the blackboard paint. Use two coats on the edges to seal them. For a tidy look, rim the board with picture-frame molding.

SELF-CLEANING SHELVES

Salt a sandbox with a collection of plastic cows and sheep and kids will soon be busy sculpting a farmstead where the animals can live. Bring in toy boats and there will soon be canals for them to sail. The only problem with lots of toys is that they can quickly clutter the sandbox, leaving no way to play without breaking something.

Building kid-height storage shelves nearby solves this problem, and also allows parents to rotate toys into and out of the sandbox so they don't grow stale. Kids are most likely to use shelving that they can see, so build open shelves, without doors. Use coated-wire shelving, typically sold for closets, so any sand that clings to the toys will fall right through.

playhouses, forts, and tree houses

FROM THE TIME THEY ARE *toddlers* all the way into their teens, children cherish private spaces where they can be in charge. Playhouses, forts, and tree houses serve this need wonderfully. Some children delight in concocting elaborate fantasy adventures. Others put their energy into decorating or enjoying a personal hideaway. The play structure should support these activities, not get in the way of them by being so fancy or so carefully decorated that children get scolded for using it. Neither should a playhouse, fort, or tree house be built without any involvement by the children. The best structures result from a team effort of kids and parents, as you will see in the following pages. This chapter explores the ways playhouses and forts differ, and discusses some of the issues to consider before you build. It also includes plans for structures large and small.

planning

Although playhouses, forts, and tree houses may seem similar except for their construction details, the play experiences they provide are actually quite different.

Playhouses, just as the word implies, are all about playing house. Kids establish roles and rules, work at decorating and tidying, and act out many daily activities. The play focuses on relationships between people inside the playhouse.

Forts, however, are all about "us vs. them," about relationships between people inside the fort and an outside enemy force—raccoons, other children, even parents.

Tree houses can serve as either playhouses or forts. Their special role, however, is to be an "away place" that only invited guests can enter.

All three types of structures lend themselves to later use by adults, if doorways and ceilings are high enough. Consider future use as you plan.

With the addition of a post or two, even a relatively small tree can support a tree house.

BUILD OR BUY?

Building a playhouse, fort, or tree house can be a lot of fun—or a nightmare that seems to go on and on. When time or skill is short, a variety of kits or ready-made solutions are worth considering.

Depending on available resources and skill level, you may want to have a playhouse built and installed for you or put the finishing touches on a prefab or partially assembled kit.

Pieces in a Kit (Prefab)
Sold at home centers as a storage shed, the precut kit shown below (left) can easily be used to build a playhouse. Kits include all lumber and fasteners but not foundation materials. Door height: 6 feet. Depending on size, a kit usually costs less than $1,000 unassembled.

Partially Assembled Playhouse Kit
The kit from Practical Folly Playhouses shown below (center) was designed for play, so it includes features such as a Dutch door and a ladder to the belfry lookout. It's shipped with floor, wall, and roof sections ready to be screwed into place. Door height: 4 feet. Many companies sell partially assembled play structures, and the costs vary widely.

Check to see if the prices you're quoted include shipping, fasteners, and a foundation.

Custom-built Playhouse
Scaled for kids but with all the bells and whistles of a standard house, this custom-built playhouse from La Petite Maison (below right) features a fully finished interior and detailed exterior with wrap-around porch. Door height: 4 feet 6 inches. High-end play houses are typically fully installed at your home and can cost about the same as for a mid-sized car.

building your own

If you don't want to choose a prefab, you can build a special play structure that suits your needs and location.

CONSTRUCTION STYLES

The construction methods described here work well for playhouses, forts, and tree houses.

STANDARD STUD CONSTRUCTION

Build a skeleton from 2 by 4s, 2 by 3s, or, for a small playhouse, even 1 by 2s. Then cover the framing with roofing and siding. This is probably the best method to use on playhouses that will later be converted to permanent structures in the garden or guest houses. If you hire builders, it's probably the method they will pick.

- Build the floor first, then frame walls on it.
- Assemble walls horizontally so you can drive nails straight through the base and top plates into studs. Install windows on the floor while walls are still flat.
- Make side walls as long as the floor. End walls should be the width of the floor minus the thickness of the two side walls.
- Prop up one side wall, nail it to the floor, and brace it diagonally so it stays upright. Then prop up an end wall and fasten it to

the floor and to the side wall. Add the other two walls.
- Build the roof in place. Start by tacking uprights to temporarily support a ridge beam. Install the ridge beam, then each pair of rafters.
- Add siding and trim.

PLYWOOD SHELL Cut sheets of plywood for the floor, walls, and roof. Add bracing where needed for stiffness or for seating fasteners. Because everything is built in panels, this method works well when a playhouse or fort is built at one location and then assembled elsewhere. It's also a good choice for a structure that will later be taken apart and moved.

- For floors, use 3/4-inch plywood or a double layer of 3/8-inch. Walls and roof can be 3/8-inch or 1/2-inch.
- Lay out walls so they make efficient use of plywood, which generally comes in sheets 4 by 8 feet. Trim the floor to fit with the wall dimensions; you'll make fewer cuts.
- Screws and nails don't hold well when they are driven into the end grain of plywood. Beef up such connections by adding a piece of solid wood (at least 1 inch by 2 inches) to the rear

plywood piece so the screw has something firm to grab.
- For easy, perfectly hung doors and window shutters, cut the plywood only along the hinge line of these openings. Stop and add hinges. Then cut out the rest of the opening.

POLE BUILDING Borrowing from a popular method for building barns, set posts into the ground and use them for both the foundation and the corner posts of the playhouse or fort. This is the easiest, fastest construction method. It's especially suitable for structures that parents frame but kids finish. Because the framing and foundation are the same, pole structures can't be moved.

- Set rot-resistant posts into the ground at least 2 feet deep or below the frost line. Secure either with concrete or sharp-edged gravel packed tight.
- Bolt rim joists onto the posts to support the floor and the roof.
- Add vertical wall framing where necessary, including on both sides of doors and windows, and frame the roof.
- Add roofing, siding, and trim.

FOUNDATIONS

A playhouse or fort doesn't need a full-scale foundation, but there must still be a way to keep the floor dry and the siding off the ground. With a tree house, the foundation is the trickiest detail. Once it's done, the rest of the construction is fairly standard.

BUILDING ON THE GROUND Setting a playhouse on an existing paved patio may seem like a simple solution. But if the paving extends beyond the walls, water will almost surely get in. Instead, give the floor an elevated foundation of some type. For maximum durability, avoid direct contact between concrete and wood.

Set the floor joists on pier blocks or standard concrete blocks (above). Fastening temporary buildings to the blocks isn't crucial because the weight of the structures holds them in place. Letting gravity do the job also makes it easier to move the building later, if desired.

For permanent structures built on the ground, a circular form to pour concrete into eases the task of constructing concrete piers that reach below the frost line.

BUILDING IN TREES Tree houses can be supported by one, two, three, or more trees, or even by trees plus posts set into the ground. Nails or screws won't hurt a tree, as long as they are not spaced closely together. But trees can be injured if a chain or rope girdles the trunk or if a tree house rubs against the bark. Because trees bend in the wind and grow wider over the years, foundations must be built to flex as needed. In a pushing match, trees always beat tree houses.

When a single tree supports a tree house, the floor or deck usually circles the trunk (below). Attach each of the two main beams to the trunk with a single bolt, or use a custom-made fitting as shown on page 79. Add rim joists, attaching them to each other but not to the two main supports so that the floor can slide as the tree grows wider. Then install diagonal bracing to keep

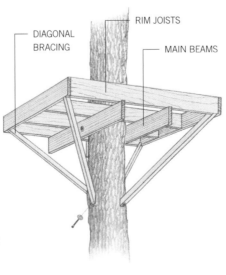

the floor from tipping. Only once those are in place is it safe to climb onto the framing and finish the floor. These details are more fully explored starting on page 76.

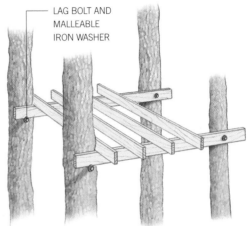

LAG BOLT AND MALLEABLE IRON WASHER

Four trees or a combination of trees and posts can be used like corner posts to support a tree house (above). Small structures close to the ground can rest on two beams bolted to the trees. Larger or higher tree houses should rest on supports that allow the base to move as the trees grow and sway in the wind. To reate a flexible foundation, bolt nly one end of each support eam to a tree. Support the other nd with a connection that allows ovement. One solution, shown n more detail on page 84, allows the support beam to rest on a large lag bolt driven only part way into the trunk. A malleable iron washer acts as a stop.

DIAGONAL BRACING

RIM JOISTS

MAIN BEAMS

materials worth considering

Besides the construction materials commonly used on houses, some items warrant special attention for use in playhouses and forts.

METAL ROOFING Inexpensive and quick to install, metal roofing looks great and lets kids enjoy the pitter-patter of falling rain. Screws with neoprene washers seal out the rain. Choose galvanized roofing if you want a rustic look or painted styles for a more finished look. Use full-length pieces if possible. If not, cut panels with a circular saw. Wear safety goggles for the glowing metal shards, ear protectors for the screech, and gloves for the sharp edges. Install so the cut edges hide under the roof cap.

FENCE BOARDS Board-and-batten walls give a playhouse or fort a pleasant, rustic look that will be especially attractive if the structure is later converted to a garden shed. Good-quality fence boards don't cost much and can work quite well, but the wood will probably still be wet when bought and will later shrink considerably. Provide plenty of overlap, and nail so that the wood can move without splitting. This style of wall is typically built with wide boards and thin battens, but you can also use boards of equal width; just leave more space between them. Provide a generous overlap—at least ¾ inch for 4-inch boards and more for wider ones. Because vertical boards absorb water along their bottom edge, increasing the risk of rot, coat those ends liberally with a water-repellent preservative to prevent it. Pick a preservative that is paintable if you plan to add a finish to the wall.

PLYWOOD WITH BATTENS Adding thin vertical trim boards to simple plywood walls dresses them up considerably and mimics the look of true board-and-batten siding. If you want to stain or paint the battens a different color than the underlying wall, apply the finishes before installation.

METAL ROOFING
Cut metal roofing with a circular saw fitted with either a special metal-cutting blade or a non-carbide blade set backward. Metal roofing flexes; provide support so blade doesn't bend.

FENCE BOARDS
If walls are less than 6 feet tall, you may be able to save money by using fence boards rather than standard lumber for board-and-batten siding. Avoid boards with loose knots, however, and be aware that fence boards may contain too much moisture to be painted right away. With any type of wood, board-and-batten siding must be installed so the boards won't split when they expand and contract as humidity fluctuates. Nail wide boards only along one edge, and leave at least a nail's width between fence boards or up to ½ inch with dry lumber. The battens will hold the other edge in place. Batten nails fit into the spaces between the wide boards.

PLYWOOD WITH BATTENS
Space the battens evenly and so that one is positioned over every joint where sheets of plywood meet. To avoid splitting thin battens and to hold both sheets in place, stagger the placement of the nails.

used building materials

Incorporating used building materials into playhouses, forts, and tree houses saves resources, gives the buildings instant patina, and helps them look like individual creations, not mass-produced toys.

Everything from lumber to stair parts can be found at salvage stores. For locations, check your phone directory or newspaper classified advertisements under "Building materials—used." Or call your local waste-disposal agency. Many maintain referral lists as a way to cut down on construction waste. See the Resource Guide for other suggestions.

As you wander through a used-building-materials store, think about how parts may be employed unconventionally. Maybe those beautiful balusters could be cut in half and turned into window trim. Or that old toilet seat could be painted and made into the frame for an oval window.

HOW TO INSTALL A VINTAGE WINDOW

Used windows and doors are often less costly and more beautiful than new ones. However, a full double-hung window may be too large for a playhouse while a single sash fits just right. Hinge the window so it can swing open. Or insert dowels through the side studs and into the window frame at midpoint so it can pivot open. Provide a cap over the window if it's not under a roof overhang, and make sure the sill angles down.

If the window hinges on the bottom, add chains on both sides to catch the weight of the window when it's open and to limit the opening.

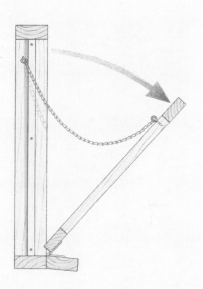

Katelyn's Kastles specializes in building playhouses with salvaged materials. An old toilet seat is converted into an "Open for Business" sign. Stair parts serve as everything from a porch railing to a ship's portal. Old shutters, windows, columns, and assorted other parts give each playhouse a look all its own.

a build-it-yourself playhouse

Some kids gravitate more toward simple structures that they can shape themselves. Four sturdy posts in the ground and an assortment of other materials give kids a way to build their own forts and playhouses.

Jeff Powers and Debby Haase outfitted an old outbuilding on their property as a playhouse, but their children rarely used it. Then Jeff framed a smaller structure and left it for Ken, 8, and Charlie, 11, to finish. Day after day, it occupied their attention as they found leftover siding for the walls and scrap plywood for the roof. When rain threatened, they even rigged up a ditch to channel water away from the structure. "With the other playhouse, there wasn't anything left for them to do," Debby says. "With this one, they did it all."

Building materials can range from old sheets and curtains to wood that's at least long enough to span the posts. The posts should be sturdy enough to withstand having a variety of things nailed to them, pulled out, and nailed back many times.

Older children may want to build on a somewhat elevated platform so they have a floor. For safe floor supports, help them bolt on thick planks, at least 2 by 6 inches. Recess the bolts (see page 17) or cover exposed ends with cap screws. Also ensure that there's a safe way up and down, if that's an issue.

BUILDING INSTRUCTIONS

Dig oversized post holes 2 feet deep or below the frost line. With a level, adjust posts so they are perfectly vertical. Temporarily brace them in place.

Add concrete or gravel, tamping after each shovelful or two with a sturdy piece of wood or metal to remove air pockets. If you don't have enough material to fill the holes, use tamped earth or gravel near the top.

Concrete makes poles more rigid, but gravel is easier to remove when the playhouse is no longer an item of interest.

GETTING IT SQUARE

Although kid-built forts don't have to be square, budding carpenters will probably appreciate posts set at right angles to one another. To do this, begin at the first post and measure out 3 feet in one direction and 4 feet at an approximate right angle. Adjust the end points until the distance between them equals 5 feet. Any point on the 3- or 4-foot lines will then be a suitable place for posts. About 4 feet apart works well (especially if you or the children will be cutting apart 8-foot boards to use for the fort itself). Locate the final post in a similar manner.

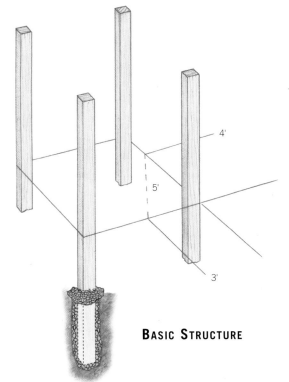

BASIC STRUCTURE

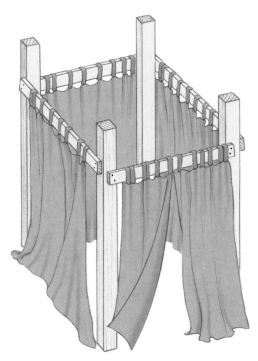

THEATER
Tie on sheets or curtains and let the kids put on a show.

FORT
Inexpensive lengths of 1 by 2s, hammered in place with 4d (1½-inch) nails, make a great kid-built fort.

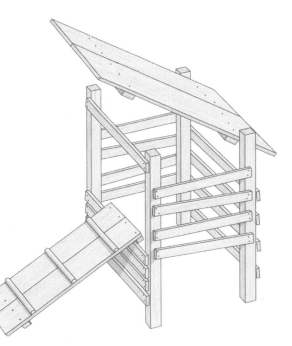

MATERIALS

- Four rot-resistant 4 × 4 posts, each 6'–8' long
- 4–6 bags of ready-mix or fast-setting concrete, or sharp-edged gravel
- An assortment of other building materials: boards, nails, palm branches, fabric, etc.

51

a cardboard playhouse

For decades, kids have recognized the potential of cardboard boxes, especially big ones. With strapping tape and an adult to help cut out windows and doors, a serviceable playhouse can easily be made. Add a few tools and pieces of readily available "hardware," however, and the possibilities expand enormously.

To create houses that are stronger and more rigid than they would be with tape alone, the most useful addition in this project is the plastic cable tie, which electricians use to bundle wires. Look in the electrical department of a home center or hardware store for packages of white or multicolored ties. Insert the ties though holes punched in a big box with a pumpkin-carving tool or an electric drill.

Cardboard strips, which are easily cut with a home-made tool, also boost construction possibilities. Use the strips to bolster connections and to straighten bends in the box.

Just as carpenters develop preferences about types of wood, cardboard carpenters soon learn to appreciate different varieties of card-board. Corrugated cardboard usually comes in single and double thicknesses. With each additional layer, the structure becomes stronger.

Wardrobe moving boxes work well because they're big and double-thick. Appliance boxes are also ideal. Packing-supply companies sell 4-by-8 sheets of single-wall card-board for less than $5. But with cable ties and cardboard strips, big playhouses can be fashioned from relatively small boxes.

BUILDING INSTRUCTIONS

1 Open up the boxes and cut through one corner so that each makes one flat piece.

2 From other pieces of cardboard, cut approximately 50 linear feet of strips 5 inches wide.

3 Arrange three boxes into a rectangle to form walls of the house. With the flaps on the bottom end pointed in, place one box so that three of its sides form one long wall and the remaining side forms part of one end wall. Use the next box so that half completes the end wall and half begins the other long wall of the house. The third box fills in the rest. Overlap the boxes as shown in the illustration so that the end wall is about 48 inches wide.

4 Using cable ties, join the three boxes. Add cardboard strips as needed to cover joints and to fortify places where the boxes were cut or bent. Before sealing up the final piece, cut the door so that one person can get inside

to thread through the cable ties. Extend the top flaps to help support the roof.

5 Cut down one box to 48 by 60 inches and lower it in as the floor. This will add rigidity.

6 Attach cardboard strips to the remaining box to turn its flaps into part of the roof.

Also add strips along what had been the box's corner bends. The strips will help keep the roof from sagging.

7 Cut the gable pieces as shown below and attach to the end walls with cable ties. Cut and bend back part of the flaps at the top of the end walls to match the angle on the roof.

8 Add the roof and attach with cable ties. Then cut out windows and paint, if desired.

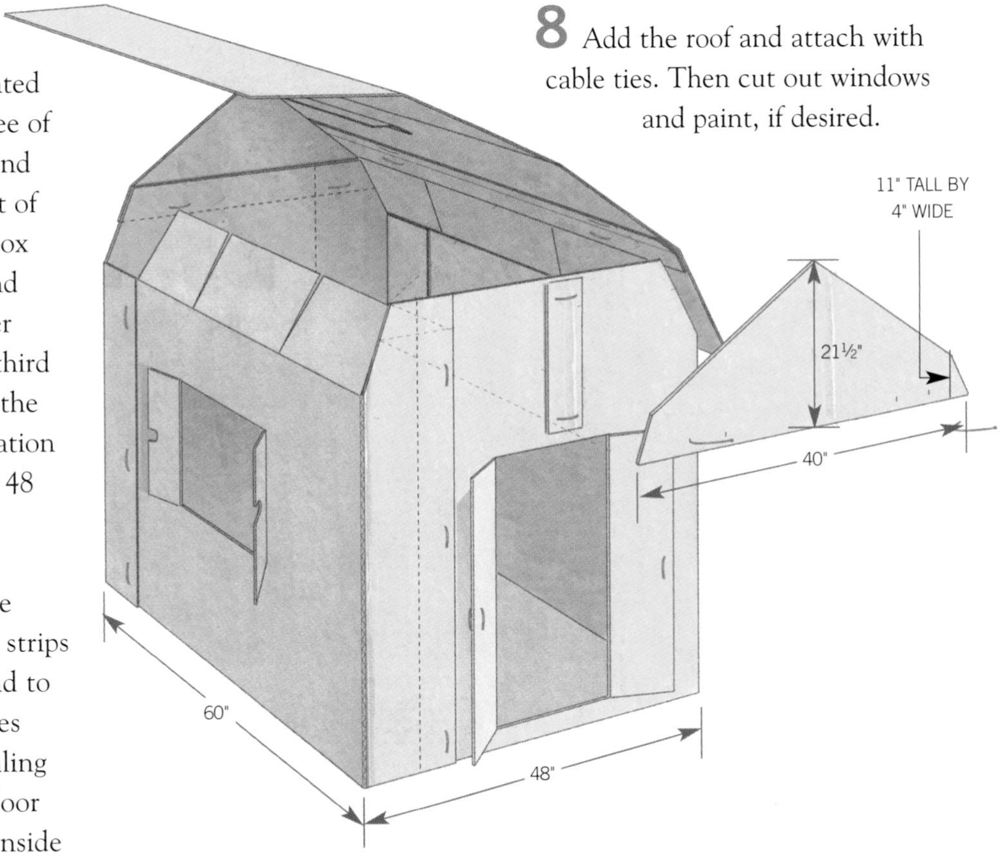

11" TALL BY 4" WIDE

21½"

40"

60"

48"

MATERIALS

- Five 20" × 20" × 46" wardrobe moving boxes
- Additional cardboard to make approximately 50 linear feet of strips about 5" wide
- Two 22" × 40" cardboard pieces
- Package of cable ties
- Latex paint, if desired

CARDBOARD CUTTING TOOLS (see page 54)

- Homemade strip cutter
- Pizza cutter
- Pumpkin-carving tools
- Hacksaw
- Circle cutter

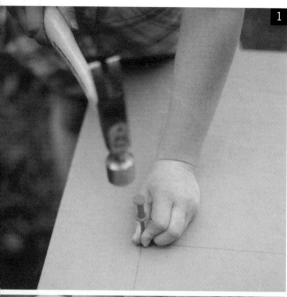

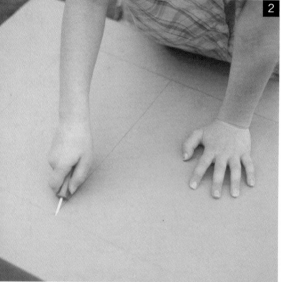

A KID-FRIENDLY WAY TO CUT CARDBOARD

Although a utility knife remains the standard way to cut cardboard, this tool is not suitable for young children to use. Pumpkin-carving tools and a hacksaw designed for use in tight spaces let kids tackle jobs that otherwise would require them to ask for adult help.

1 Sophia, 7, starts cutting out a window by creating holes at each corner. She hammers in a pick designed for piercing a pumpkin shell.

2 She then uses a pumpkin-carving saw to cut a slot about ¾ inch long.

3 After slipping the hacksaw blade into the slot, she saws around the opening. The hacksaw blade has smaller teeth than the pumpkin-carving tool, so it's easier for her to use.

TOOLS FOR BUILDING

Cardboard carpenters go through lots of strips, circles, slotted cross-pieces and cable ties. Simple tools speed the work.

A. A strip cutter can be made from four foot-long pieces of wood, two about ¼ inch thick and two about ½ inch thick. Cut slots in the two thin pieces so that short bolts screwed into wing nuts can slide down the openings. In each thick piece, cut two grooves to match the width and thickness of the thin pieces. Glue and nail one end of each slotted piece to one of the thick pieces, and drill into the other thick piece so that you can slip in the bolts with the wing nuts. Two tiny pan-head screws, which are flat on the back, hold a utility-knife blade at an angle. Use the cutter over a surface that can be cut into. A workbench covered with extra sheets of cardboard or inexpensive particleboard works well. Kaza, 13, discovered that it's important to press down firmly with both hands. Loosen the wing nuts to adjust the width of the cardboard strips.

B. To join sections with a cable tie, drill two holes using a bit about ¼ inch wide. Insert the tie and pull it tight.

C. A pizza cutter is useful in making creases to bend cardboard. Press down along a straightedge to create a valley that bends easily into a crisp corner.

D. To make a circle cutter, drill a hole through a piece of scrap wood the width of a craft knife handle, stopping slightly short of going all the way through. Hammer the knife (with blade attached) into the hole so that the blade is perpendicular to the wooden arm and the tip projects as far as the cardboard is thick. The tip of a drywall screw serves as a pivot point. Evan, 9, presses down on the pivot screw as he moves the cutter around in a circle. Like the strip cutter, this tool must be used over a surface that can be cut into.

E. A hacksaw equipped with two blades spaced to match the thickness of cardboard efficiently cuts slots that allow strips to interlock. Adding a cardboard X to the interior of a small box strengthens it enough to serve as a playhouse chair.

OUTFITTING A PLAYHOUSE KITCHEN

Older children enjoy making playhouse furniture for younger children to play with. A playhouse kitchen makes a fun project.

- To create a sink cabinet, cut a circle in one end of a cardboard box and slip in a small stainless-steel bowl.

- For a stove, paint two cardboard circles black and glue them onto the end of another box.
- For a refrigerator or a cabinet under the sink or the stove, cut door flaps in one side of a box and add a sturdy shelf (see picture C above). For a shelf that's strong enough to hold toy dishes, cut a piece of cardboard about 1½ inches wider in all directions than you want the shelf to be. Use the excess to make flaps that bend down and attach them to the sides of the cabinet with cable ties. The bent-down flap at the front will help keep the shelf from sagging.

a Lincoln Log playhouse

Inspired by old-fashioned Lincoln Log construction sets, this playhouse can be assembled or taken down easily and quickly, making it ideal for families who want a temporary playhouse.

The "logs" are milled cedar decking boards, with smooth surfaces and rounded-over edges. They need virtually no sanding, which speeds the work in making this playhouse. So that the parts can be left outdoors, notches are slightly oversize; even if the wood swells because of moisture, the pieces will still slide together easily. If you want to mimic the worn look of antique construction sets, leave wall pieces unpainted but tint the roof red. Sponging on a light coating of ordinary latex paint and then immediately wiping off any excess will allow the wood grain to show through.

The hut photographed here is about 4 feet long and 3 feet wide. Max and Avery, twin 5-year-olds, had no problem lifting the pieces and fitting the walls together. Their mom helped with the roof.

For a more spacious playhouse, simply cut longer pieces or make more for higher walls. As with any construction set, the more pieces, the greater the options and the more creativity the builders can show. Providing just a few pieces of many different lengths isn't as useful as having multiple pieces of fewer lengths, however. In a large set, the parts will be most versatile if some are half the length of others, or if some are one-third and others two-thirds the length of long pieces. Calculate the base length from the center of one notch to the center of the next.

When you cut the wood, add 5 inches to the nominal length to account for overlapped ends.

This version uses angled pieces for the gable ends of a peaked roof. Because the roof gets high and the parts are slightly tricky to install, you might want a simpler roof if young children will be building this house on their own. Set aside the roof boards and instead use extra wall pieces. Place them horizontally so their notches lock into the walls. To complete this simpler roof, toss a blanket over the boards.

BUILDING THE JIGS

Creating a Lincoln Log–style play set requires cutting dozens of notches that line up with each other. Although the notches can be cut by hand or on a table saw with a dado blade, the work goes quickly and easily with a router and a jig that allows 10 or more notches to be cut at once.

The basic jig, used for cutting notches in the main wall pieces and end stubs, includes a bar that aligns the ends of the boards so you can run a router down one side and up the other to create a wide notch. You'll need a modified jig to cut notches in the gable-end pieces. To accommodate their angled shape, the bar that aligns the ends must also be cut on an angle. Locate fences for this jig to create notches that have their centerlines 5 inches from the ends of the boards. This allows the notch in the short side of one gable piece to line up with the long side of the gable piece above.

Jig Detail

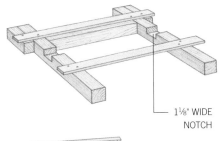

1⅛" WIDE NOTCH

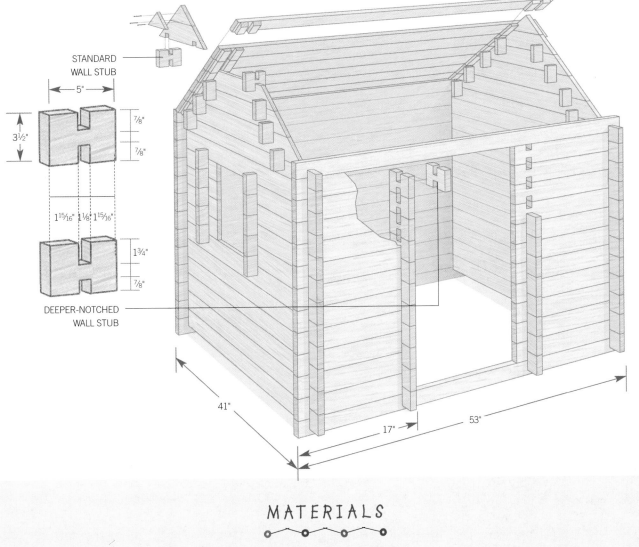

STANDARD WALL STUB

5"

3½"

⅞"

⅞"

1¹⁵⁄₁₆" 1⅛" 1¹⁵⁄₁₆"

1¾"

⅞"

DEEPER-NOTCHED WALL STUB

41"

17"

53"

MATERIALS

- Decking boards: 15 pieces ⁵⁄₄ × 4 × 12', 14 pieces ⁵⁄₄ × 4 × 8'
- Two cedar strips, 1 × 2 × 8'
- Wood glue
- About sixty 1⅝" finish nails
- A few ounces of paint, if desired

CREATING THE PARTS

Just a few simple steps, repeated over and over, create the parts for this playhouse. Accuracy matters, so begin by checking the ends of boards. If they aren't perfectly square, trim them. Then cut all the big pieces.

From each 12-foot piece, cut two pieces 53 inches long and two pieces 17 inches long.

From ten of the 8-foot deck boards, cut two pieces 41 inches long. Then cut one of the 41-inch-long pieces to make two pieces 17 inches long.

Use two of the remaining 8-foot deck boards and scraps from the steps above to make the 5-inch stubs. But don't cut them to that length yet or the jig won't work. Instead, cut them to double-length: 10 inches plus the width of one saw blade.

Cut the remaining two 8-foot deck boards at a 45-degree angle to create the gable ends. Sandwich the boards together and cut a pair of pieces 36 inches long (long point to long point, with both ends angled out at the bottom); then make three succeeding pairs, each 7 inches shorter than the one before. Use two of the 10-inch pieces you already created to make the triangles for the top of the gable ends, as shown in the illustration on page 57.

After following these steps you should have:

- 29 boards 53 inches long (four of which will be trimmed width-wise by $\frac{7}{8}$ inch after notches are cut)
- 19 boards 41 inches long
- 32 boards 17 inches long
- 52 wall stubs 5 inches long (12 of which will need to have a deeper notch on one side)
- 5 pairs of gable pieces

Set aside 14 of the 53-inch pieces to use on the roof and cut notches in both ends of all the other pieces.

1 Line up as many pieces as will fit in the jig. Clamp the jig to the pieces as well as to a workbench. Using a straight bit ($\frac{1}{2}$-inch works well) in a router, cut the groove by making several passes, each no more than $\frac{1}{4}$ inch deep. Work down one fence and up the other, then direct the router freehand down the center to clean out any wood remaining in the notches. With $\frac{5}{4}$-by-4 decking boards, which measure a full 1 inch thick, a notch about $1\frac{1}{8}$ inches wide and $\frac{7}{8}$ inch deep works well.

2 A dozen of the 5-inch stubs needed for this playhouse must have a deeper groove ($1\frac{5}{8}$ inches) on one side than the other so that the stubs can link logs even when their notches don't line up (such as at the top and bottom of windows). Cut the deeper notches with a handsaw and chisel out the waste.

3 Roof boards need small cleats at the ends so they fit over the gable ends and lock into place. Cut the 1 by 2s into pieces $3\frac{1}{2}$ inches long, making a 45-degree angle on one end of eight of the pieces (for the two ridge boards, see step 7). To ensure perfect alignment, place a notched wall "log" next to the roof board and line up the cleat with the notch. Tack the cleat in place by driving nails only slightly through. Then remove the cleat, add glue, reposition, and finish nailing in place.

ASSEMBLING THE PLAYHOUSE

After you've prepared all the pieces, there are two final adjustments to make. Cut a strip ⅛ inch wide off the edge of four of the longest wall boards. Two of these strips will be used in the bottom course of logs, and two will be used at the top. Also, add a small triangular piece to the top gable piece (see step 7) to hold it in place.

Assembling the playhouse is straightforward, and kids catch on fast. Use the 5-inch stubs to keep boards lined up at the doorway and the window. Choose stubs with the deeper notch for the bottom and top of the door, the window, and the transition from wall to gable end.

4 Finish each of the long walls with a board that has been trimmed to remove one set of notches.

5 Use stubs with deeper notches to attach the first gable-end piece to the wall. Notches on the remaining gable pieces line up so that you can use stubs with the standard ⅞-inch-deep notches.

6 With two gable-end pieces set, snug the first roof boards into place. The cleats fit over the gable ends. The top wall piece acts as a stop to keep the roof from slipping off.

7 There is no space for a stub at the top of the gable end. Instead, nail on a small triangular piece to provide a lip. The ridge roof boards, with their angled cleats, lock everything in place.

a princess playhouse

Isabella, 3½, loves to pretend she's living a fairy tale. So when planning for her playhouse began, the design seemed obvious: It should be a castle!

Adults involved in this project began discussing ways to mimic a stone fortress. Then one of the fundamental points about designing kids' play spaces kicked in: Isabella was asked what *she* had in mind. It wasn't a castle in the traditional sense. Instead of stone walls, the little girl imagined a round tower painted purple. This delightful octagon is the result.

Round or octagonal buildings can be tricky to build. But this ingenious structure is quick and easy. The roof is the biggest short-cut. It's an eight-panel market umbrella, which fits nicely over the building's octagonal shape. The walls consist of plywood trimmed with quarter-round molding to fill the spaces between the panels. The window shutters and doors are cutouts from the walls, adding to the simplicity. Heavy gate hardware gives the castle a slightly mysterious look.

The playhouse is designed for use on a deck or patio. Because these spaces usually serve multiple purposes, the building is easy to disassemble and put back up again. The wall sections are held together with door hinges that have removable pins. Taking down the structure is as simple as popping out the pins and carrying away the plywood. The entire structure breaks down into one folded-up umbrella plus a stack of plywood 2 feet wide, 5 inches thick, and 5½ feet long.

The walls are 5½ feet high because those proportions seemed pleasing. However, this height means that a few inches needed to be cut off the umbrella pole so that the roof rests on the walls. To avoid having to cut off the pole, adjust the wall height to match the pole.

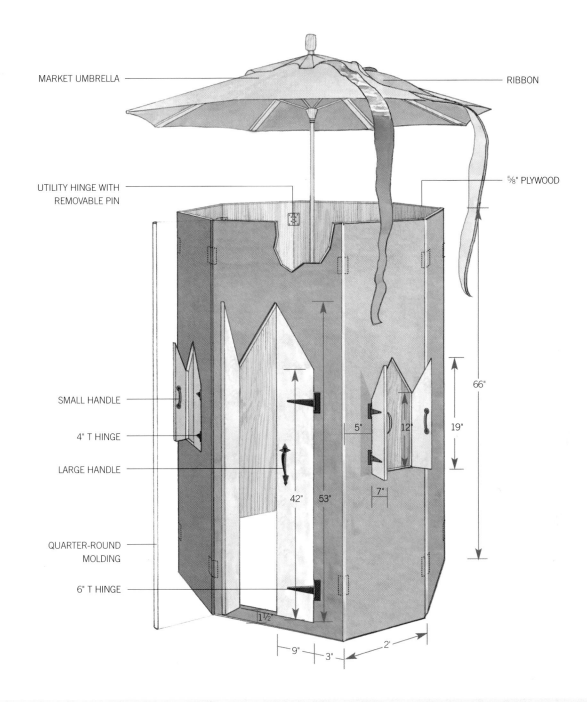

MARKET UMBRELLA

RIBBON

UTILITY HINGE WITH
REMOVABLE PIN

⅝" PLYWOOD

SMALL HANDLE

4" T HINGE

LARGE HANDLE

QUARTER-ROUND
MOLDING

6" T HINGE

66"

19"

5" 12"

7"

42" 53"

1½"

9" 3" 2'

MATERIALS

- Eight-panel 7' market umbrella
- Four sheets ⅝" ACX plywood
- Sixteen 3" utility door hinges with removable pins
- Eight pieces ⅝" quarter round, each 5'4"
- Finish nails, 1¼"
- Four 6" black gate T hinges (for door)

- Eight 4" black gate T hinges (for windows)
- Four black handles (for windows)
- Two black gate handles (for door)
- Paint
- Ribbons or other accessories, as desired

2 To create perfectly hung shutters or doors with little effort, install hinges before you make the final cuts. Be sure to align the hinges so that the guide on the saw will rest flat on the plywood for all cuts. Or switch to a jigsaw, which has a smaller footprint. (Remember to remove the door and window hardware before you paint. Re-attach them once the paint dries.)

3 Door hinges with removable pins hold the wall sections together. To enable easy reassembly of the panels, even if all hinges aren't at exactly the same height, number the panels before you install the hardware. To keep the project from becoming unwieldy, remove the pins from each pair of panels once hinges are in place. This way, you'll be working with only two panels at a time. The hinges go on the inside of the structure.

4 When all the hinges are in place, pin the wall sections back together in pairs and set them upright. They will stay up on their own. Then couple the pairs together to form the full octagon.

BUILDING THE WALLS

Because this playhouse is designed to go on a deck or patio, it needs no other foundation or floor. There is no framing, either. Instead, the walls are cut from $\frac{5}{8}$-inch plywood. A good choice is ACX, an exterior plywood with one smooth, knot-free "A" face and one slightly blemished "C" face. The playhouse requires eight wall panels, each $5\frac{1}{2}$ feet tall and 2 feet wide.

1 Cut window and door openings and create the window shutters and doors at the same time by using a circular saw. Set the blade depth to the thickness of the plywood. Start the cut by tipping the tool backward so that no teeth touch the wood. Turn on the saw and gently lower it into the cut while the blade is spinning. Cut along hinged edges, then stop. You can also cut out the windows and door with a jigsaw. Drill a hole as wide as the blade at each corner before you cut.

5 Quarter-round molding fills the gaps between panels in the octagon. Attach the molding with glue and nails. Nail sideways through the molding to pin it to only one wall section. Be sure not to nail into both wall sections or into the space between the panels. Attach molding strips to the same side of each wall section so that every panel winds up with one trim piece.

6 Set up the umbrella at the center of the playhouse. If there is a gap between the umbrella and the walls, measure it and trim the post by that amount. Or, if the umbrella has a sectional pole, remove the lower part, open the umbrella, and rest it on the walls. Prop the lower part of the pole next to the upper section. The overlapping area should be cut away. Once assembly is complete, paint the walls, doors, and windows.

7 Trimmed with ribbon, the umbrella pole becomes a decorative feature of the playhouse interior. An umbrella support stand is not needed because the umbrella's weight rests on the walls.

8 When you want to dismantle the playhouse, the pins may be difficult to remove. An easy way to free them is to hammer a slim nail up into the barrel.

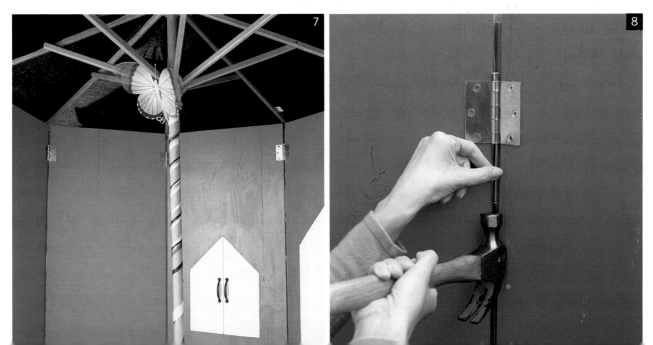

teepee for two

Easy to put up and take down, this teepee makes a great portable fort or playhouse for young children. And it's simple enough to create in less than half a day.

This teepee is made mostly of ripstop nylon, the same material often used for windbreakers. Besides being colorful, it sheds rain reasonably well and dries fast. Decorative details, made from cotton applied with an iron-on adhesive, reinforce areas where shoelaces are threaded through grommets to hold the fabric to bamboo poles.

Prepare each pole by hammering a steel rod into the wide end until only about 4 inches of metal projects. Drill a $\frac{1}{4}$-inch-wide hole all the way through the bamboo 62 inches up from that end. Thread the long shoelace

through all holes, joining the poles together. Knot the lace so there is little slack.

Mark and cut the fabric as shown in the illustrations on the opposite page. Apply the decorative details by following directions provided with the iron-on adhesive, which is sold at fabric and crafts stores. Insert grommets, using the tool packaged with them. Five grommets go on each zigzag at the teepee opening. Place the first one $\frac{1}{2}$ inch down from the top and $\frac{3}{4}$ inch in from

the edge. Set the others every $2\frac{3}{4}$ inches. Also place a grommet in the center of each small circle of trim. With a hole punch, make two holes in each triangle of trim at the bottom of the teepee (about $\frac{1}{2}$ inch up from the edge) and 15 holes through the triangles at the top. Start the top holes $1\frac{1}{2}$ inches from the opening edge and space them 1 inch apart.

Use two of the remaining shoelaces as ties for the door. Thread them part way through the grommets on the small circles. Weave one shoelace through the holes at the top of the teepee. Cut the rest of the shoelaces in half and knot the cut ends. Thread one lace through each of the punched holes so both ends will be inside the structure.

ERECTING THE TEEPEE

To set up the teepee, first mark off a circle 5 feet in diameter. A piece of string tacked to a stake works well as a compass. Mark six points approximately equal distance from one another. (Divide the circle in half, then divide each half into thirds.) Crossing the tops of the poles, push one post into each of these locations. Use the ends of the shoelace at the top to lash the poles tightly together to make the framing more rigid. Drape the fabric over the poles, tie it in place, and stake the tent to the ground, using the bottom ties as loops. Tie open the door so kids can run in and out.

HOW TO MARK AND CUT FABRIC

1 Fold the material in half crosswise, so the two cut ends line up. Starting at one of the corners with a fold, use a tape measure or piece of string as a compass and mark two arcs: one at 5 inches and one at 5 feet. Mark where the diagonal intersects the arcs. Also mark the large arc 15 inches in from the edge without the fold and 15 inches in past that. Continue the pattern and transfer marks to the bottom layer until the full half-circle is evenly divided into 12 segments. Cut out the fabric and finish the curved edge, using either a sewing machine's zigzag stitch or a hand-done blanket stitch.

2 Cut trim pieces and adhesive sheets as shown:
- Two circles 8 inches in diameter
- Two circles 1½ inches in diameter
- Two zigzags 12 inches high and 3 inches wide; keep shaded small triangles for teepee's top edge
- 12 large triangles 3 inches high and 1½ inches wide

3 Apply trim. Place small circles 22 inches from the bottom and 11 inches from the front edge. Large circles go about 10½ inches farther in (measured from center points). Cut one large triangle in half and bond one piece at the bottom of each front edge. Apply the others at the spots marked on the bottom arc. At the top of the teepee, place seven of the small triangles point to point along the edge. Bond. Then partially overlap a second row of six small triangles.

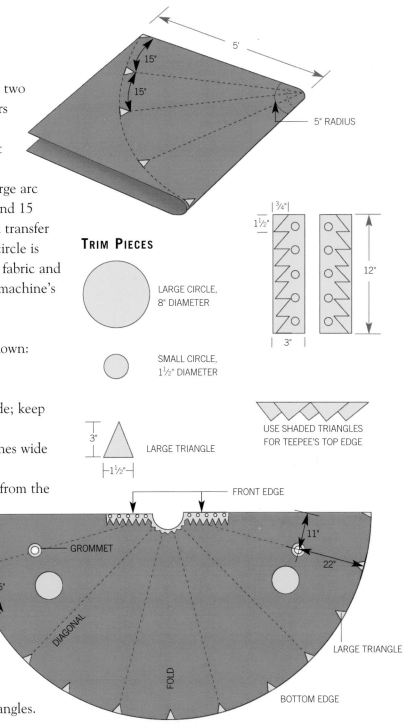

TRIM PIECES

LARGE CIRCLE, 8" DIAMETER

SMALL CIRCLE, 1½" DIAMETER

LARGE TRIANGLE

USE SHADED TRIANGLES FOR TEEPEE'S TOP EDGE

FRONT EDGE

GROMMET

LARGE TRIANGLE

BOTTOM EDGE

DIAGONAL

FOLD

MATERIALS

- **Ripstop nylon: 3⅓ yards 60" wide**
- **Cotton for decoration, ½ yard 45" wide**
- **Iron-on adhesive (see Resource Guide), 1 yard**
- **Twelve ¼" grommets**
- **Nine 27" shoelaces**

- **One 54" shoelace**
- **Six bamboo poles, 1" × 8'**
- **Six steel rods, ¼" × 1'**
- **Six tent pegs**

a Norwegian cabin

Designed to be a playhouse now and a potting shed later, this cute little cottage was inspired by a family's memories of several pleasant years spent in Norway.

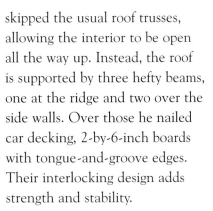

Many a quaint Scandinavian outbuilding has a sod roof and a board ceiling, and so does this playhouse. Lucky, the 7-year-old girl for whom this house was built, helped carry and spread the sod, which she sees as a potential habitat for her pet frog. Other homespun details include recycled leaded-glass windows, two of which were kitchen cabinet doors in their original life, and a Dutch door, which was fashioned from an old two-panel door.

It can be tricky to design a kid-size playhouse that has enough headroom for adult use. Several features of this building help to minimize its size while maximizing its space. Bob Stanton, the carpenter who designed and built the structure, skipped the usual roof trusses, allowing the interior to be open all the way up. Instead, the roof is supported by three hefty beams, one at the ridge and two over the side walls. Over those he nailed car decking, 2-by-6-inch boards with tongue-and-groove edges. Their interlocking design adds strength and stability.

Without trusses, Stanton needed something to pin the walls in place to keep them from bowing out because of the roof load. He stabilized the structure by nailing a few of the roof boards to the top framing piece on the end walls, adding diagonal bracing and mortising studs into the top plate of each side wall. The added joinery gives the structure some of the feel of a timber-frame building, but with cuts that are easy to make.

Use of a sod roof helps keep the playhouse from looking too big on the outside. The peak isn't very high because sod would slide off a steep slope. And, of course, there's all that greenery, which makes the playhouse look like part of the garden—perfect for a playhouse destined to be a potting shed.

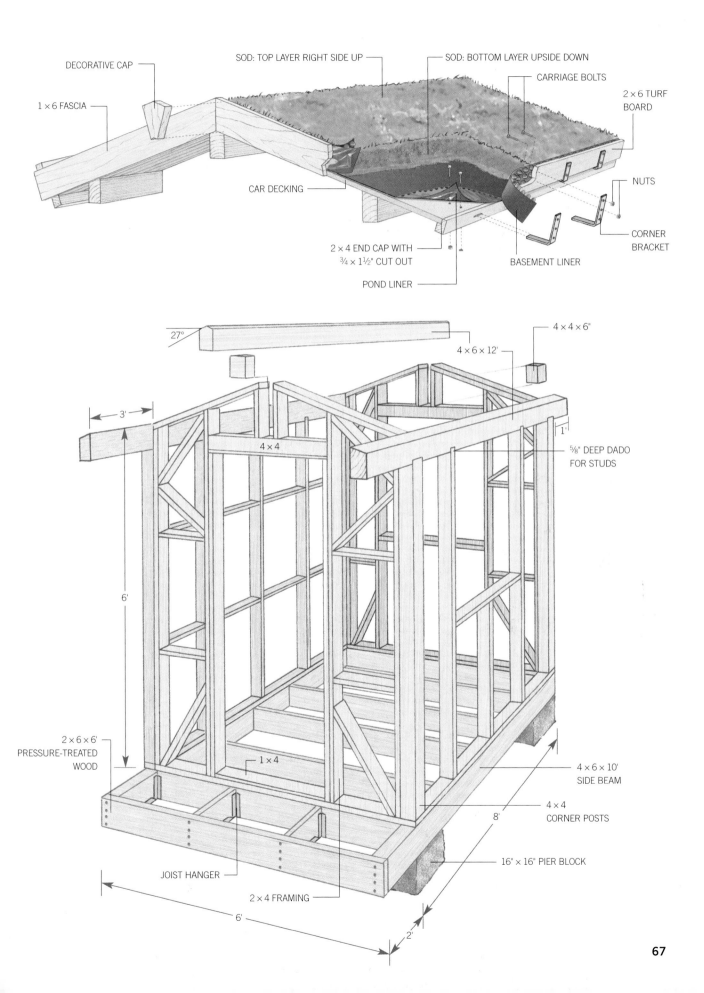

DECORATIVE CAP

1 × 6 FASCIA

SOD: TOP LAYER RIGHT SIDE UP

SOD: BOTTOM LAYER UPSIDE DOWN

CARRIAGE BOLTS

2 × 6 TURF BOARD

NUTS

CORNER BRACKET

CAR DECKING

2 × 4 END CAP WITH
¾ × 1½" CUT OUT

POND LINER

BASEMENT LINER

27°

4 × 4 × 6"

4 × 6 × 12'

3'

1'

⅝" DEEP DADO FOR STUDS

4 × 4

6'

2 × 6 × 6'
PRESSURE-TREATED WOOD

1 × 4

4 × 6 × 10'
SIDE BEAM

4 × 4
CORNER POSTS

8'

JOIST HANGER

2 × 4 FRAMING

16" × 16" PIER BLOCK

6'

2'

BUILDING INSTRUCTIONS

1 The foundation consists of four concrete pier blocks recessed into the ground enough so that their top surfaces are level. Joist hangers and nails hold the 4-by-6-inch side beams to the rest of the floor framing. Joists are doubled under end walls of the cabin. The plywood floor (one full sheet and one half-sheet cut lengthwise) fits flush with the outside perimeter of the framing.

2 Three substantial roof beams add to the traditional feel of this playhouse and allow the truss-free roof. Preparation begins by cutting ⅝-inch-deep mortises for the side-wall studs. The easiest method is to first make multiple passes with a circular saw, leaving approximately

MATERIALS

FLOOR

- Four 16" × 16" pier blocks
- Two 4 × 6 × 10' pressure-treated beams
- Nine 2 × 6 × 6' pressure-treated joists
- Twelve joist hangers for 2 × 6s
- 1½ sheets of ¾" exterior plywood, such as ACX
- Decking material to cover 6' × 2' deck (boards to run in 6' lengths)
- Galvanized nails, 3"

ROOF

- Three 4 × 6 × 12' beams
- Fifty-two pieces 2 × 6 × 5' car decking
- Two 2 × 6 × 12' rot-resistant turf boards
- Four 1 × 6 × 6' rot-resistant fascias
- Two 2 × 4 × 12' end caps
- One sheet pond liner, 12' × 14'
- Basement water-channel liner, enough for two panels each 5' × 12'
- Sod, 240 square feet
- Duct tape, 12 feet
- Eight 6" galvanized corner brackets
- Thirty-two ⁵⁄₁₆" × 2" carriage bolts with nuts
- Galvanized nails, 2½"

WALLS

- Framing: 25 pieces 2 × 4 × 8'
- Corners and miscellaneous: two pieces 4 × 4 × 12', one piece 4 × 4 × 6'
- Windows, as desired

SIDING

- Boards: 27 pieces 1 × 8 × 6', 14 pieces 1 × 8 × 8'
- Battens: 27 pieces 1 × 2 × 6', 14 pieces 1 × 8 × 8'
- Corner and trim boards: 11 pieces 1 × 4 × 10'
- Door and jam
- Windows
- Galvanized siding nails, 2½"
- Galvanized nails for framing, 3"

¹⁄₈ inch between cuts. A chisel quickly cleans out the waste.

3 Taking advantage of the flat floor, Stanton drew out the roof details. The roof's 28-inch rise from side wall to ridge determines the angle of the roof. The beams need to be beveled to match that slope, but most circular saws don't cut deeply enough to accomplish the job in one pass. This mock-up shows how he cut the side beams. He tacked a guide piece onto the beam and made the cut shown on the left. Then he flipped the beam over and cut through the rest of the way to wind up with the piece on the right. If the cuts weren't made in this order, he would not have had enough wood to support the saw on the final cut.

4 Stanton framed the walls on the floor, ensuring a perfect fit. The side walls run the full length of the floor; the end walls equal the width minus the space needed for the side walls. Because this playhouse will have board-and-batten siding, the framing includes 2-by-4-inch blocking at two

heights. If plywood siding were used, blocking would not be necessary.

5 After building both side walls, Stanton nailed the board-and-batten siding to the back wall, then tilted it into place. With diagonal bracing holding the wall steady, he nailed through the bottom plate to secure the wall to the floor. Then he raised and braced the other side wall. A row of nails finishes this step.

6 There is no framing per se for the roof except along the end walls, where 2-by-4-inch braces keep the roof weight from pushing the side walls apart. The length of these pieces is also easily determined by measuring the full-scale roof drawing made in step 3.

7 Stanton trims the car decking boards to length and to the roof angle. Instead of doing it piece by piece, he lines up several planks and cuts through them all at once. Car decking is typically sold in 10- or 16-foot lengths, so one set-up can yield a dozen of the 5-foot pieces needed for this roof.

8 After trimming off the groove edge on the end pieces, Stanton nails the car decking into place. For most of the pieces, nails go only into the beams. But over the end walls, Stanton also nails the car decking to the top brace piece in the wall framing.

9 Board-and-batten siding must be attached in a way that allows it to expand and contract as humidity fluctuates; otherwise the wood will crack. First, Stanton nails the boards in place, leaving a nail's width between each board. He pins down only one edge of each board, placing a single nail 1 inch in at each level of horizontal framing. Batten nails fit into the gaps between boards and hold down the free edges of the boards (see page 48).

INSTALLING THE SOD ROOF

Traditional sod roofs consist of multiple layers of birch bark covered by two layers of turf, one placed grass side down and the other grass side up. Today, the turf layers remain the same but a variety of modern materials replace the bark. Products used for waterproofing basement walls work well.

For this playhouse, a plastic pond liner big enough to cover the entire roof serves as a waterproof membrane. A dimpled plastic sheet, sold primarily for basement work (see Resource Guide), is laid over that. The dimples create an airspace on the back and give the grass roots something to grip to on the front. A network of little channels formed in the plastic directs rainwater off the roof. See the illustration on page 67 for more information.

10 In Norway, special brackets are available to hold up the board that keeps turf from sliding off the roof. These brackets have a bulge that allows the waterproofing material and the water-channel layer to extend past the edge of the roof deck. To get the same result with materials commonly available in this country, Stanton cut out small ovals in the roof end cap and slipped 6-inch corner brackets through. Then he used a small piece of each of the plastic materials as a template for aligning

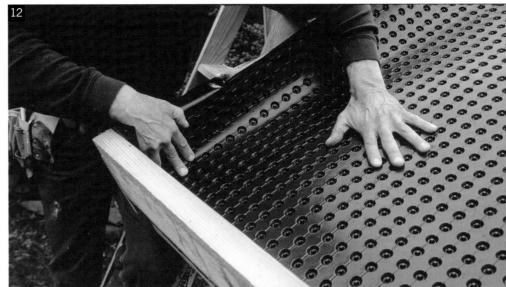

the brackets. He set the gap between the turf board and the roof wide enough to allow both plastic layers to fit underneath.

11 With the turf board in place, Stanton draped the water-proofing layer over the roof and pulled up the front and back edges to cover the 1-by-6-inch fascia pieces on the eaves. To keep the membrane from flopping down, he tacked it in place along the eaves only. The main roof expanse has no fasteners, so nothing compromises the waterproofing.

12 The basement waterproof-ing layer came in a roll. Stanton cut two pieces, one for each side of the roof, and then smoothed them in place. At the ridge, he taped the pieces together with duct tape. At the bottom, he pushes the plastic down so that it extends past the edge of the roof deck and touches the metal brackets. The membrane curls up at the eaves, protecting the wood there. Cutting a separate strip for the eaves is another option.

13 Sod arrives from a garden center in pieces that unroll just like carpet. The first layer goes grass side down; the top layer grass side up. Arrange the layers so that joints do not overlap. For the first layer, begin with a piece cut in half crosswise. For the sec-ond layer, start with a piece cut in half lengthwise. Tuck in roots along the edges as you go to avoid a patchwork look.

14 After the turf settles in, fill in any gaps with handfuls of soil. Scatter grass seed and add seeds of low-growing wildflowers if you wish. In areas where summers are dry, poke bits of sedum or other succulents into the sod. They will root and spread, allowing the roof to remain green or multicolored (depending on which varieties you select) even during drought. Sod roofs don't need to be mowed, but they may need to be raked every few years to remove excess thatch.

stockade fort with lookout

This fort serves as a Wild West hangout one day and a clubhouse the next. And when kids outgrow their interest in concocting fresh fantasies there, the fenced-in space can be converted to utilitarian purposes, such as storing wheelbarrows, recycling bins, and other bulky items.

Because space was tight in this yard, the stockade is just 8 by 8 feet, with a lookout 4 by 4 feet. Where space allows, the fort can be made larger. The structure is easy to build. The stockade goes together almost like a fence, and the lookout is basically a small elevated deck with a roof on top.

Embellishments, such as the flagpole and peephole, help boost the play value. To protect neighbors' privacy, the lookout has solid boards over both back walls. In the lucky situation where playmates are just over the fence, installing a second ladder or a clothesline mail-delivery system out the back might be worth considering.

One safety note: The lookout has a single safety rail 2 feet high. If very young children will be using the space, think about raising the rail and adding vertical pieces between it and the floor. Be sure to keep gaps to 3½ inches or less.

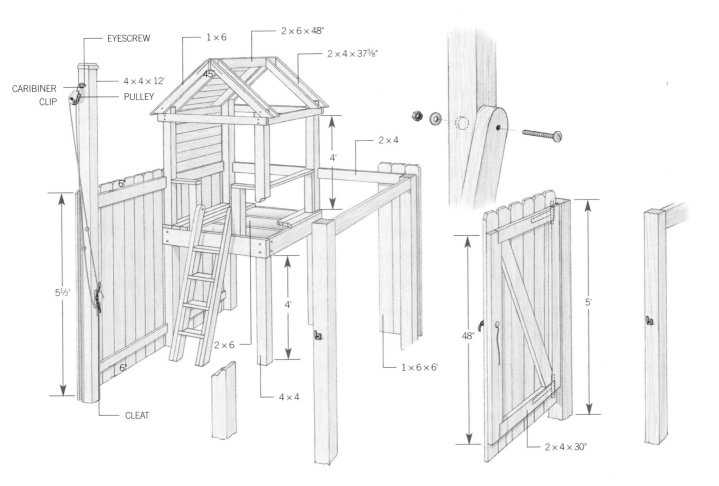

Figure labels: EYESCREW · CARIBINER CLIP · PULLEY · 1 × 6 · 2 × 6 × 48" · 2 × 4 × 37⅜" · 4 × 4 × 12' · 45 · 4' · 2 × 4 · 5½' · 6' · 4' · 4' · 2 × 6 · 4 × 4 · 1 × 6 × 6' · CLEAT · 6' · 6' · 48" · 5' · 2 × 4 × 30"

MATERIALS

STOCKADE AND FLAGPOLE

- Posts (includes excess for railing), six 4 × 4 × 10', one 4 × 4 × 12', one 4 × 4 × 8'
- Approximately twelve 60-pound bags concrete mix
- Eight rails, 2 × 4 × 8' (includes gate rails)
- Eighty fence boards, 1 × 6 × 6' (includes 6 for gate)
- Galvanized nails, 3½" and 1¾"
- Fence post cap
- Three eyescrews, ⅜"
- Rope, 15'
- Caribiner clip
- Pulley
- Cleat

GATE

- Frame pieces, two 2 × 4 × 4', one 2 × 4 × 5'
- Two 6" T hinges
- Gate latch with string

FLOOR

- Six joists, 2 × 6 × 4'
- Four joist hangers
- Twelve ½" × 5" carriage bolts, with lock washers and nuts
- Fourteen decking boards, 2 × 4 × 8'
- Galvanized deck screws, 2½"
- Joist hanger nails

ROOF

- Framing: six 2 × 4 × 8' (cut to make 4 pieces 4' long and 8 pieces 37¾" long with ends angled 45° with both tips out)
- Ridge beam, 2 × 6 × 48"
- Fourteen fence boards, 1 × 6 × 6'
- Four carriage bolts, ⅜" × 7", with nuts and washers

RAILING

- Two posts, 4 × 4 × 2' (use excess from stockade posts)
- Rails, one 2 × 4 × 4', two 2 × 4 × 16"
- Four carriage bolts, ½" × 5", with nuts and washers

LADDER

- Three pieces 2 × 4 × 8', cut into two stringers 67" long, four treads 13" long, and eight tread supports 9" long with ends angled 15°
- Galvanized deck screws, 2½"
- Two galvanized carriage bolts, ½" × 5", with nuts and lock washers

PEEPHOLE

- Threaded rod, 8-32, 12" long
- Two cap nuts, 8-32
- Two no. 8 lock washers
- Machine screw nut, 8-32

BUILDING INSTRUCTIONS

1 A little advance planning helps this play structure go together easily. The first step might seem like it should be done at the end, but doing it at the beginning eliminates a top-of-the-ladder job later. Install hardware for the flagpole while the post is still flat on the ground. Standard flagpole pulleys attach directly to the post. Or, as shown here, use an eyescrew, caribiner clip, and standard pulley.

2 Set the posts after determining the width needed for the gate: the width of six nice fence boards plus $\frac{1}{2}$ to $\frac{3}{4}$ inch of swing space plus whatever gap is needed for the hinges. When the posts are in place, notch into the two that are at the back of the fort at the height of the floor of the lookout (4 feet). The joist there needs to fit into these grooves to put the back walls of the fort on the same plane as the fence boards around the stockade. To cut the grooves, make multiple passes with a circular saw. Chisel out the waste.

3 The fence rails go in next. They are toenailed in place with 3$\frac{1}{2}$-inch galvanized nails. To keep the rails aligned while driving the nails at an angle, tack or clamp a block of scrap wood underneath.

4 Floor joists are held in place with metal hangers. Special hanger nails have the thickness needed for strength but are short enough to stay embedded within the wood. When the lookout framing is done, nail on the floor and then stand on it to build the roof. To create a base for the roof, nail four 4-foot 2 by 4s horizontally to the posts 4 feet above the floor. Nail rafters in pairs to this base along the side walls and to the ridge beam. Two pairs of rafters go on the outside of the main posts and two go on the inside, creating somewhat of a Craftsman look. Lock the assembly in place by threading a 7-inch carriage bolt through the post and the two rafters at each corner.

5 A sturdy ladder has treads supported by wood, not just nails or screws. Either cut grooves at an angle that will allow the treads to sit flat, using a procedure similar to that for cutting grooves in the posts in step 2, or, as shown here, cut angled supports and fit them against the ladder rails between each tread. Screw the parts together.

6 The gate's top and bottom rails are notched into the side framing pieces, and a diagonal brace guards against sagging. The brace, which must fit precisely, runs from the top on the latch side to the bottom on the hinge side.

7 Because of their T-shape, the gate's hinges need to be aligned with the top and bottom rails of the framing. The easiest way to hang a gate is while it consists of just the frame and the board or two that will fit under the hinge. The rest of the boards can be nailed on while the gate is in place.

8 For a fun detail, create a 2-inch-wide peephole with a door-knob hole saw. Cut out a 3-inch circular cover with a jigsaw. Swing the cover back and forth over the hole to locate the best position for a pivot. Then drill a $\frac{3}{16}$-inch hole through the cover and the fence. Screw a cap nut and a lock washer onto one end of the threaded rod and insert it through the fence board. Add another lock washer. The peephole cover and the other cap nut complete the setup. The cover should swing freely so that it closes on its own.

a tree house built by pros

The TreeHouse Workshop specializes in creating airborne offices, guest quarters, and other adult retreats. But for this project, the company set out to construct a children's tree house simple enough to be built by people who relish challenging weekend projects, such as building a deck or a potting shed. Unlike many backyard tree houses, this one is super-sturdy and built to last for years.

Because no two trees are the same, it's unlikely that you will be able to copy this plan exactly. But the basic steps—and solutions—are those that work for most tree house projects.

The first hurdle is to decide which tree or trees to use. For this project, the family favored two towering Douglas firs, one with two trunks, about 12 feet from their back deck. Some branches were dead, though, and sap oozed from one trunk. So they did what anyone contemplating a hefty treehouse would be wise to do: They called in an arborist. The sap wasn't problemmatic, but the dead branches were removed and the live ones were thinned to enable wind pressure against the trees and the tree house to approximate the pressure that used to push against the trees alone.

Locating the tree house in these trees turned out to be a brilliant move, because the easy access encourages frequent use. But one lesson from hindsight: prune a season in advance, especially in springtime, to minimize sap drips onto your tree house.

Kids' tree houses come to life when they incorporate design ideas generated by the children who will play there. The lucky owner of this tree house, 9-year-old Eric, sketched out a medieval-looking tree house with tall, thin windows flanking a heavy door with iron hardware. Over the center of the roof, he drew a lookout tower for spying on kids using a neighborhood trail. But building a rooftop tower would have complicated the job enormously. So the TreeHouse Workshop crew came up with a plan for a separate crow's nest, which was built later (see page 84).

Eric was disappointed when he found out how high the tree house would be—just 8 feet off the ground at the front, on the high side of a slope. But when the job was done, Eric was thrilled. Tree houses don't have to be very high to be magical places.

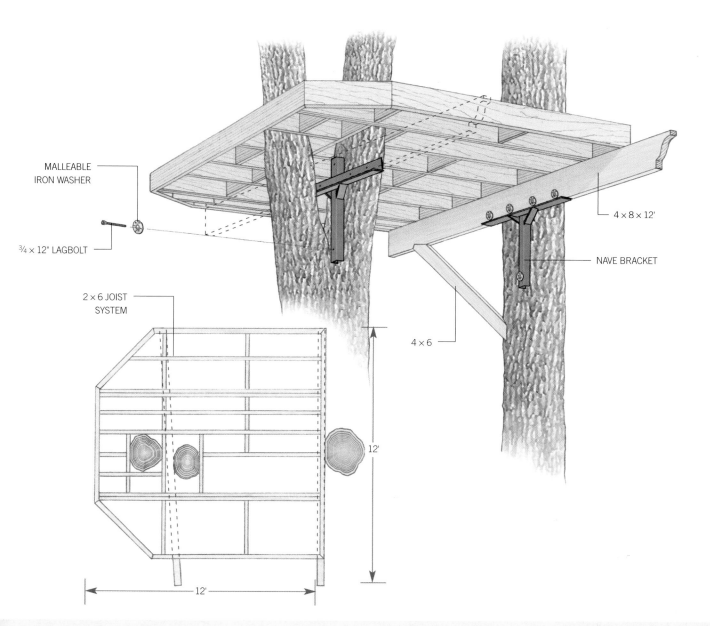

MALLEABLE
IRON WASHER

¾ × 12" LAGBOLT

2 × 6 JOIST
SYSTEM

4 × 8 × 12'

NAVE BRACKET

4 × 6

12'

12'

MATERIALS FOR DECK

For a two-tree deck approximately 12 by 12 feet:

- Two nave brackets (see details in step 2)
- Six galvanized lag bolts, ¾" × 12"
- Eight galvanized bolts, ⅝" × 5", with nuts and malleable iron washers
- Two Douglas fir beams, 4 × 8 × 12'
- Two braces, 4 × 6 × 10'
- Douglas fir joists, thirteen 2 × 6 × 12', two 2 × 6 × 8'
- Twenty-five pieces rot-resistant decking, 2 × 6 × 12'
- Deck screws, 3" (20 pounds of screws were used for the tree house, bridge, and lookout)

For the deck trim and railing:

- Four cedar boards, 1 × 8 × 12'
- Four cedar planks, 2 × 6 × 12'
- Eight cedar pieces, 2 × 4 × 12'
- Ten posts, 4 × 4 × 8'
- Approximately 125 sturdy branches, each 30½" long and at least 1½" in diameter

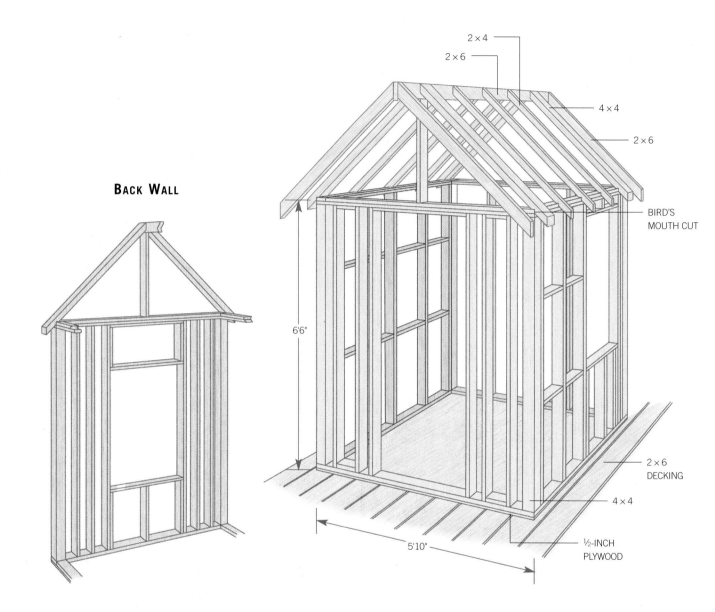

BACK WALL

2 × 4

2 × 6

4 × 4

2 × 6

BIRD'S
MOUTH CUT

6'6"

2 × 6
DECKING

4 × 4

½-INCH
PLYWOOD

5'10"

MATERIALS FOR TREE HOUSE

For a tree house approximately 6' × 6':

- Studs: eight 2 × 4 × 14', seven 2 × 4 × 12', five 2 × 4 × 10'
- Framing pieces: one 2 × 6 × 8', two 4 × 4 × 10', two 4 × 4 × 14'
- Twenty-two exterior boards: eight 1 × 10 × 14', fourteen 1 × 10 × 8'
- Cedar battens, 1 × 2, same lengths as boards
- Exterior plywood, 3½ sheets ½"

- Metal roofing to cover two sides, each approximately 4' × 7', with roofing screws and ridge cap

This project used recycled windows and an old door cut down to 2' × 6'. The materials listed here are needed for a tree house with just that door opening. For each window you add, you will probably need two or three additional 2 × 4s. Adding these will reduce the number of board-and-batten pieces you need.

THE KEY COMPONENT

The biggest issue in building a tree house is attaching it to the tree or trees so the house stays up and the trees aren't damaged by excessive rubbing into the nutrient-carrying layer directly under the bark. Although it may sound complicated, the easiest way to accomplish both goals is to order custom T-shape supports from a metal fabricator or welding shop. The TreeHouse Workshop refers to these pieces as "nave brackets" because their shape follows the floor plan of medieval cathedrals in Europe. This tree house needed two supports, which cost about $100 each.

1 To create a template for the fabricator, Jake Jacob of the TreeHouse Workshop straps a 40-inch-long 2 by 4 along the central axis of the trunk. Then he levels and screws on a 2-by-4 crosspiece at the height of the lowest edge of the tree house deck structure. This produces a template adjusted for the tree's slant.

2 Following the template, the fabricator created this nave bracket. The vertical piece is a 40-inch length of 3-inch steel channel ($\frac{3}{16}$ inch thick). The crosspiece is a 48-inch length of 3-inch angle iron (also $\frac{3}{16}$ inch thick). These pieces are welded into a cross arranged so that the upper section does not project beyond the height of the deck. Steel triangles welded to the main

pieces provide reinforcement. A $\frac{3}{4}$-inch hole at each end of the vertical piece and four holes along the crosspiece allow the fitting to be bolted to the tree and to the deck supports.

3 After establishing one tree as his reference point, Jacob straps a nave bracket in place and drills pilot holes for the two ¾-inch galvanized lag bolts that will tie the metal to the tree. He uses a long auger bit in a half-inch drill equipped with handles, a professional setup available from tool-rental companies. To do the job with homeowner-scale tools, drill as far as possible with a spade bit, then add a bit extension and continue drilling to the depth needed for the bolts.

4 To establish the position of the second nave bracket, a crew member straps a 2 by 4 to the bottom of the first bracket and extends the wood to the other tree. Using a level, he fine-tunes the 2 by 4's position, then temporarily screws it in place. He repeats this process with a second 2 by 4 on the other side of the trees. Then he and the rest of the crew hoist the second nave bracket and bolt it in place.

5 With both nave brackets attached, a crew member bolts on one of the 4-by-8 support beams. The shelf created by the angle iron makes this step easy as long as all the holes line up properly. The malleable iron washers (see Resource Guide) provide more bearing surface than ordinary flat washers and look a bit fancy.

BUILDING THE SUPPORT STRUCTURE

Using the special metal supports and staying within ladder height of the ground allows the tree house support structure to go together almost like a deck. A two- or three-person crew speeds the work and reduces the number of trips up and down a ladder. Building a support structure is not a job for children, however. Be especially wary of allowing them to be where things might fall on them.

6 The deck rim, made of 2-by-6 Douglas fir, comes next. Instead of nailing the framing, a crew member uses 3-inch ceramic coated deck screws. (See Resource Guide for the style this crew favored.) When you're working on a ladder, a drill gives you more control than a hammer does, and parts stay aligned better.

7 Before adding the rest of the framing, the crew pauses to install two diagonal braces that help shift the tree house weight directly back to the trees. Figuring out where to cut is tricky because the top must be inset slightly into the beam while the base needs to fit perfectly flush with the bark. To create a template for the top cut, the crew snapped a chalk line onto stiff paper and then copied the shape onto the beam.

8 The lower edge of the diagonal requires only a simple angle cut and perhaps a little judicious paring of the bark so that there's a flat place for the end to rest. Shallow cuts into a small section of bark won't harm the tree. To keep the tree's moisture from wicking into the brace, the crew slipped a piece of mudsill gasket material into the joint and then attached the brace to the tree with a 12-inch galvanized lag bolt.

9

10

11

decks. And, of course, the tree house is located up in the air. Plan the work so that you can stand on the ground or on the platform whenever possible. Working on a ladder is not only more dangerous, it's more time consuming and it's harder on your body.

9 After installing a network of 2-by-6 joists spaced approximately 16 inches apart, the builders proceed to screw on 2-by-6 deck boards. These will serve as flooring for the outdoor areas and as a subfloor for the interior.

10 A liberal zigzag of construction adhesive around the perimeter of the floor, and at spots in the middle, seals the plywood floor to the decking and prevents rainwater from being pushed inside by wind. The decking alone would be plenty strong for a tree house floor, but the plywood was added because Eric hopes to add carpet to the interior.

BUILDING THE DECK AND THE TREE HOUSE

Once the support structure is built, the job proceeds much like any deck-construction project, then shifts to steps similar to those for building a garden shed. There are a few differences, however. Because this deck also supports the tree house, joists need to be sized according to flooring span charts, not those generated for

11 The crew framed the first wall on the ground and then lifted it onto the platform, where they installed the window. It's easiest to build everything on the ground, but the weight can become too much for a few people to lift without the help of pulleys and ropes. Doing the work partly on the ground and partly on the platform proved easiest in this case.

12 The tree house's two side walls nearly abut the trees. So the builders installed the board-and-batten siding and exterior window trim before they fixed the walls in place.

13 When the side walls were up, the crew framed the end walls and then built the roof. After nailing a king post to each gable end, they hoisted the ridge beam and nailed on the rafters. "Bird's mouth" indentations in the rafters provide secure footing against the top plate. Using metal rafter ties instead would simplify this step.

14 For the railing, the family used some of the branches trimmed from the fir trees and supplemented them with cedar branches, also from their property. Because branches are never straight, Jacob built a jig that allows each piece to settle into its natural alignment. The jig also makes it easy to cut each piece exactly to length. A screw through each end secures the pieces to the railing framing. For a sturdy railing, use only sound branches that are at least 1½ inches in diameter and space them 3 inches apart.

A CROW'S NEST LOOKOUT

For spying on anyone using a trail below or for launching pine cones against "the enemy," the best spot in the neighborhood is this crow's nest, which fits right between the double trunks of a towering Douglas fir. Although it was built as an add-on to the tree house featured on the previous pages, a project such as this could also serve as a small stand-alone tree house.

Instead of using the custom steel brackets that support the tree house, the TreeHouse Workshop attached this overlook to the tree with four 1-inch-wide galvanized lag bolts 12 inches long. The bolts are screwed only part way into the tree, allowing the excess to provide a perch for the floor framing. Malleable iron washers serve as stops that lock the platform into place. One critical detail with this system is that the bolts must be long enough to penetrate solid wood, not just bark.

Framing for the floor consists of 4-by-8 beams half-lapped where they intersect. The ladder leads to a trapdoor in the floor, a detail that saves space and adds fun.

Above: The crow's nest perches on four thick bolts and malleable iron washers, available at industrial-supply companies. The bolts provide a perch, and the washers create a lip that keeps the tree house from sliding. *Left:* Eric's crow's nest rises over the deck of his tree house. The deck acts as a safety feature because it protects against the possibility that a child could fall all the way to the ground. *Below:* The trapdoor, about 2 feet square, opens in the middle. Holes cut into two of the decking boards serve as handles.

A CLATTER-BRIDGE ENTRY

Although a simple ladder works fine as a way to get up and down from a tree house, a clatter bridge adds tremendously to the fun. This bridge, which links the tree house to the family's deck 12 feet away, has been used to launch water balloons on people passing by. Kids tie bird netting to it to see what they can catch below. And, of course, children running on a clatter bridge generate a lot of noise.

A bridge such as this must start and end at approximately the same level. To get up to the level of the tree house floor as well as to clear the rail around the family's deck, the builders installed a ladder on one end of the bridge. Diagonal braces serve as a handrail for the ladder and also help bolster the bridge's support posts, which are set into concrete. Cutouts in the decking allow the diagonal braces to run underneath the deck and tie into its support structure. On the tree house end, the chains pass through holes in the rim joist of the deck and are bolted to the next joist. With all the bouncing, strong connections at both ends are very important.

Manila rope 1½ inches thick serves as a handrail on the bridge. Because the bridge isn't very high and because the children who play here are well past the toddler stage, the family elected not to fill in the space under the rope.

Top: Eric's tree house is easily accessible from the family deck.
Above left: *The bridge rests on two thick galvanized chains. Carriage bolts ½ inch thick thread through the links to secure the 2-by-12-inch planks. Bolts through the links also secure the chains to framing at either end of the bridge.*
Above right: *The builders used pressure-treated 4 by 4s set into concrete to anchor the bridge at the deck end. To hide the incised wood, they boxed over it with beveled cedar boards.*

Where more security is desired, one solution is to string a second rope low down and then weave diagonally to create netting between the two ropes.

a quick, simple tree house

In just one weekend, Bryan Johnson hammered together this tree house for his kids, Garret, 9, and Autumn, 5. Astute streamlining speeded up the work.

The first big time saver was building in a grove of slender conifers spaced conveniently close together. Johnson found three trees about 5 or 6 feet apart, so he needed to add just one 4-by-4-inch post to have four corner posts.

Construction zipped along because the tree house is only 4 feet off the ground, freeing Johnson from needing a ladder for most of the work. He used fast pole-framing techniques (see page 46). And he skipped what usually seems an essential step: building walls. Instead, he erected a simple deck supported by the three trees and the post. Then, higher up on the same supports, he built a roof. The floor and the roof float independently, yet create what seems to be a full tree house because Johnson filled in the railings with siding boards.

Johnson tried to make the floor somewhat square, but didn't worry about making it exactly that. When he got to the roof, however, he needed a nearly perfect rectangle or the ⁵⁄₄-by-12 cedar roofing boards wouldn't line up properly. One tree outside the floor wound up being inside the roofline, so he cut into a few roof boards to accommodate the trunk. He added no other roofing, figuring that rain would blow in through the sides of the structure anyway.

The tree house may not be as sturdy or long-lasting as some, Johnson says, but his investment in both time and money was small and the play value is great. He figures that the tree house will last at least as long as his kids' interest in it. As the trees grow, they may squeeze the building, causing the floor or roof to buckle. But because the tree house is so low to the ground, there shouldn't be any safety issue.

MATERIALS

For a tree house approximately 5' × 6':

- Four trees or a combination of trees and posts 4 × 4 × 10½'
- Concrete or gravel for post holes, as needed
- Galvanized nails, 2½" and 3"

DECK

- Supports: five 2 × 8 × 6', two 2 × 8 × 5'
- Fourteen floorboards, 2 × 6 × 5'

ROOF

- Beams: two 2 × 6 × 5', three 2 × 6 × 6'
- Framing: two 2 × 4 × 3', four 2 × 4 × 4½'
- Fourteen cedar boards, ⁵⁄₄ × 12 × 4½'

RAILING

- Eight pieces 2 × 4 × 8', cut as needed
- Trim pieces: four 1 × 3 × 6', two 1 × 3 × 5', two 1 × 3 × 2½'
- 8" bevel cedar siding: eight 6', four 5', four 2½' (approximately 80 linear feet)

STAIRS

- Two 2 × 10 stringers, with ends angled 75°
- Five treads, 2 × 6 × 2'

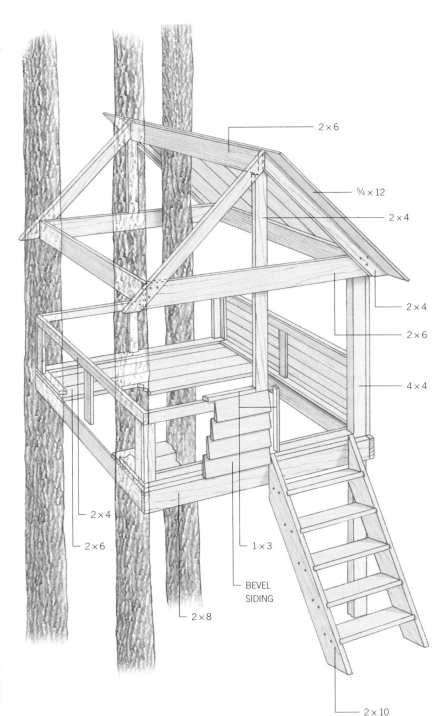

2 × 6

⁵⁄₄ × 12

2 × 4

2 × 4

2 × 6

4 × 4

2 × 4

2 × 6

1 × 3

BEVEL SIDING

2 × 8

2 × 10

MAIL-DELIVERY SYSTEM

An old-fashioned clothesline with pulleys works well as a mail-delivery system for a tree house or other play structure. Just make sure the line won't be at head height or lower for anyone who crosses the route. Install one pulley at each end of the route and connect them with a loop of cord. Clothespins clipped to the cord can carry simple notes. Bundle small treasures in recloseable plastic bags.

WINDOW BOXES

Window boxes dress up a play-house and encourage children to discover the delights of gardening. Because everything is contained in a small space, weeds aren't much of a problem and all of the action, from growing fluffy flowers to watching visiting butterflies, is close by.

This clever window box, designed by Dave Bennett of Poulsbo, Washington, has no bottom, so excess water drains straight out. There's no chance that it will dribble down the side of the playhouse, causing the siding to stain or rot. Plants fit into a removable plywood tray, cut with circles sized to the pots. This makes it easy to swap plants as flowers come into season or fade past their prime. The plywood tray sits on wooden blocks attached to the sides of the box.

WELCOME SIGN

Decorative touches help signal to kids that a playhouse or fort is really for them. Make a sign by painting a piece of wood, or create a carved look by gluing letters made for home-address markers onto a board. Use signs to name a play structure, or as a prop for a make-believe store. Have kids create their own menu, price list of stuffed animals for sale, or a changeable daily activities list on an outdoor chalk-board.

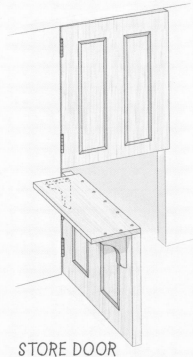

STORE DOOR

Cut a playhouse door in half and install a simple shelf on the top of the bottom half to create a surface that can be a store countertop one day, a mail center or puppet stage the next.

For this project, it's important to select a solid-wood door that has a wide piece of wood going horizontally across the middle. Saw through this wood to separate the door into two halves, taking care to miss the hole needed for the knob. Screw wooden or metal brackets into the door to support the shelf. Locate them so that the top of the shelf will be flush with the top of the door section. Screw the shelf board down into the brackets, and add a few screws that go horizontally through the door and into the shelf. A 6-inch board (which is really 5½ inches wide) works well.

PLAYHOUSE HEATER

Soapstone has a remarkable ability to absorb and hold heat, which is why it has long been used for masonry stoves. Even a small piece of this talc-rich rock can store enough heat to make a playhouse more fun on a chilly day.

Soapstone has become quite popular as a high-end countertop material, so you may be able to obtain a small piece left from a sink cutout. The material is heavy—a typical countertop thickness of 1¼ inches weighs about 19 pounds per square foot—so don't get too big a piece.

Sculptors also use soapstone as a carving medium because it's relatively soft. An art-supply store, particularly one that specializes in sculpting materials, may have chunks available. Soapstone kitchenware, pizza oven tiles, and bed warmers are other sources. Natural soapstone outcroppings occur in many parts of the country, and collecting small amounts can be the focus of a fun family outing (see Resource Guide).

The stone itself can withstand heating to very hot temperatures, but for kids' use as a playhouse heater, it should not get too hot. Use good judgment. Wrap the stone in a towel or use potholders to carry the hot rock into the playhouse, and set it on a trivet. The stone can be reheated and reused indefinitely.

PERISCOPE

To sneak a peek over walls of a fort without being detected, nothing beats a periscope. This clever tool is basically a tube with two mirrors, each fastened at a 45-degree angle. Light goes in the top, bends at the mirror, heads down to the other mirror, and bends again to get to the viewer's eyes. Periscopes can be carried around or mounted to the wall of a fort. A pivoting mount allows maximum viewing range. For the most fun, install one on each wall of the fort.

swings and play structures

MENTION "PLACES TO PLAY" AND IT'S A safe bet that most people will assume you're talking about swings, climbing frames, and other structures that promote active exercise outdoors. Young children love the thrill of sailing through the air on a swing and of conquering the fear they have a second before they let go and slip down a slide. Older ones spend hours whooshing off bike or skateboard ramps. Whatever the age, the point is to have fun, let off steam, and, along the way, hone one's judgment skills. This requires play equipment that is designed to be both safe and fun—the focus of this chapter. Most families who invest in backyard play structures opt for a manufactured system of some sort. The following pages include a guide for shopping for these systems. There are also ideas for build-it-yourself projects that promote active play. Some of the best were designed by kids themselves.

planning

Generations of children got their exercise by climbing trees and jumping off rocks. With adults rarely present to warn about what wasn't safe, kids had glorious fun. Sometimes they got hurt. Over time, they learned how far they could push themselves.

Today, many kids search for the same opportunities on swings, climbers, slides, tunnels, clatter bridges, fire poles, balance beams, and more. At some homes, kids play on this equipment daily. At others, it mostly sits unused. Why the difference?

Sometimes it's the equipment. Structures that incorporate several elements, one of which is a playhouse or fort, tend to be used more than those with a single purpose. Features that tend to be most popular include back-and-forth swings, climbing structures, tunnels, and balance beams. Young children love slides, but once the thrill of mastering them fades, so does their interest.

It's safer—and more fun—to replace outgrown features with those more suited to the age of the children. As you plan a play structure, look for ways it can be adapted as children grow. Even the simplest structures allow some changes, such as swapping kiddy swings for standard ones. But other possible adjustments, such as replacing a short slide with a spacious climbing wall, may be limited by the structure's size.

BOOSTING PLAY VALUE Many parents invest in swing sets or other play structures because they are tired of seeing their children watching television for hours on end. Merely placing outdoor

The presence of other children, not fancy features, is what brings backyard play equipment to life.

equipment in a yard usually isn't enough to get kids outside, however. The best lure is other children. In neighborhoods where kids don't meet up automatically, parents may need to spend at least as much energy linking up kids as they do lining up equipment.

Once children are outdoors, a few fresh props help to light up their imaginations. Try providing toy parachutes to launch, a stopwatch, music, or a sprinkler to run through. Planks, boxes, sheets, and other building materials also spark creativity.

LOCATING PLAY EQUIPMENT
Backyard play structures take up a lot of space, especially once the recommended safety zones are included. In small yards, consider forgoing swings, which require the largest clear zone of all play equipment, or keep them low so that the safety zone can be smaller.

Opt instead for features such as climbing walls or tube tunnels, which require very little space. Also consider play equipment that does double duty, such as balance beams that serve as garden walls.

While it's hard to adapt some structures to new uses once they've outlived their play value, it still makes sense to think of the future when the location is being selected. Play structures that survive in good condition are relatively easy to take apart and pass on to another family, leaving the original owners with a big expanse of sand, gravel, mulch, or other playground surfacing. With a little added topsoil, the old play area can become a superb garden bed. Or with a few workbenches, it can be ready for an artist's studio or a potting shed.

safety considerations

There's been so much publicity about playground safety that you might wonder if adding a backyard play structure is courting disaster. But in actuality, the risks are lower and some easier to deal with than you might think. While children have been injured or killed while playing on home play sets, several measures help reduce the risk of serious injury.

LIMITING THE HEIGHT When children don't have as far to fall, they usually don't get hurt so badly. Lowering the height of play equipment is the easiest and most effective way to increase safety. The "fall height"—the maximum height from which a child might tumble—is what matters, not the roof height. If the maximum fall height of all playground equipment was reduced to less than 5 feet, the number of children who need emergency care after playground injuries could be reduced by almost half. Relatively low heights are especially important for young children—more than a third of all children injured on home equipment are younger than 5, and their injuries tend to be to the head and face.

ADDING PROTECTIVE BARRIERS Guardrails, which are open at the bottom, keep children from inadvertently falling off elevated platforms but don't keep them from deliberately scooting underneath. Thus, they allow children to make some decisions about what they can safely do and what they should avoid. Guardrails are suitable for surfaces at a medium height: 20 inches and higher for preschoolers and 30 inches and higher for older children.

Full protective barriers, designed so kids can't get through, are needed for high spaces. That means anything over 30 inches for preschoolers and 48 inches for older children.

As with other features on play equipment, guardrails and protective barriers should be designed so they can't trap a child's head. All openings must be less than $3\frac{1}{2}$ inches or greater than 9 inches. Require children to take off bicycle helmets before they go onto play equipment, and make sure drawstrings on clothing are removed. Safety standards that guard against head entrapment don't take helmets into account, so wearing them actually increases the risk of head entrapment. Drawstrings can catch, causing a child to be dragged by a swing or injured in numerous other ways.

PROVIDING ADEQUATE CUSHIONING The softer the landing, the lower the risk of severe injury when

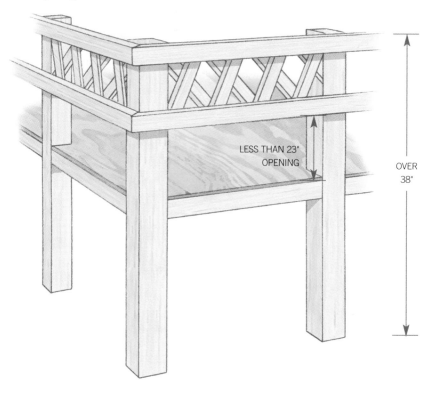

Guardrails protect both tall and short preschoolers if the rails are at least 29 inches tall and have an opening no more than 23 inches deep. For older children, the minimum guardrail height is 38 inches; the maximum opening is 28 inches.

LESS THAN 23" OPENING

OVER 38"

children fall. That's why safety experts always recommend a thick layer of sand, pea gravel, wood chips, or other material under and around play equipment. Lawn, although it shows up often in glossy brochures for play equipment, isn't sufficiently forgiving.

The issue of safety cushioning isn't as simple as installing the right material, however. It's important for children to recognize that the cushioning guards against severe head injures but will not necessarily protect against broken limbs or other injuries if the equipment is used inappropriately.

Also, for the cushioning to work as intended, it needs to be installed at a depth suitable for the height of the play equipment. To keep the material from drifting off into other parts of the yard, a system, such as earth berms or wooden beams, is needed to contain it. Excavating the area and then backfilling with the right amount of mulch also works as long as rainwater does not puddle there.

Regular maintenance is needed because most cushioning materials work by incorporating a considerable quantity of air. To remain effective, they may need to be fluffed up periodically and redistributed so that bare spots don't develop in heavy-use areas, such as the push-off space under swings. Wood products gradually decay and need to be replenished.

SELECTING CUSHIONING MATERIAL

- With wood mulch or wood chips, a depth of 9 inches or more protects children against life-threatening injuries from falls of 7 feet or less.
- With sand or pea gravel, 9 inches protects against falls from 5 feet or less.
- For play equipment less than 4 feet high, 6 inches of any of the above types of protective cushioning is sufficient. (Material less than 6 inches deep is too easily displaced.)
- With manufactured materials such as engineered wood fibers or rubber granules, ask to see results of testing according to the industry standard, "ASTM F1292". The report should list the heights of play equipment appropriate for specific amounts of the material.

- Mark the correct depth on play equipment's support legs. This helps you see when cushioning material needs to be replenished or redistributed.

LAYING OUT SAFETY ZONES

Soft surfaces clear of obstructions should extend 6 feet out from all equipment from which children may fall. Three situations demand extra attention:

Slides: The 6-foot rule applies except at the bottom of the slide. There the safety zone should equal the height of the slide plus 4 feet. Slides higher than 10 feet don't need a landing zone greater than 14 feet, however.

Standard swings: Because swings tempt children to pump as high as possible and then jump out, the safety zone must be large. To save space, lower the swings.

Tire swings: The safety zone is basically a circle with a radius equal to the chain height plus 6 feet. Kids may climb end posts, so 6-foot safety zones are needed there, too.

HEIGHT

6'

2x HEIGHT OF SWING SET

SAFETY ZONE

For swings, the safety zone in front and back should be twice the height of the pivot point.

selecting a play set

To boost backyard fun, many families opt for a play set. Besides the simple swing sets of yesteryear, equipment these days often includes a fort, a slide (or two), monkey bars, and climbing features such as nets or simulated rocks. Selecting the best structure for a particular family often involves considerable expense and many choices.

Smart planning begins by examining how your children play and how you expect that to change over the years. If your yard regularly attracts groups of children, a large play structure may be a worthwhile investment. But many families discover that backyard equipment tends to be used most when children are young. Then kids graduate to playing ball, building forts, and spending time on other activities. If you anticipate this happening in your family, spend your play-set dollars on features that will engage the interest of children while they are young, rather than invest in features that may become useful in the future.

Be sure to factor in the other play opportunities available. If a neighborhood park is nearby or your kids are in full-time day care, they may already have plenty of opportunity to swing and slide—and in settings with the bonus of other kids. Less-structured play opportunities that are messier and more self-directed may be what they can only get at home.

Although it may seem counter-intuitive, relatively simple play sets often wind up being as much fun in home settings as those that are more elaborate. The reason is that no matter what the features, play equipment tends to grow stale when it is available day after day. Then kids invent their own play opportunities—which is the point of play, anyway.

COMPONENTS, LUMBER, AND A PLAN

Lumberyards and home centers sell kits with plans that allow families to build their own play sets from standard lumber. Features such as swings and slides and their hardware may be sold individually, allowing a choice between products that are inexpensive but lightweight and those that are more expensive but also more durable.

The price of lumber is usually not included in the kit price, but sales staff are equipped to tell you the price of all the wood and components needed for each model. (Lumber prices fluctuate, so total play set prices do, too.) Be aware that some stores automatically calculate the price based on a certain type and quality of wood. You still have the option of selecting whatever type you want, although possibly at a higher price, but you may need to bring that up yourself.

The Titan play set by Swing-N-Slide is one example of a build-it-yourself kit. This design uses a 4-by-6 swing beam and 4-by-4 posts.

With this type of kit, you do all the cutting, drilling, smoothing, and staining. The process is spelled out for you, however, and the play equipment typically is designed to be easy to build, with special metal fittings to eliminate the need for fancy joinery.

These kits tend to be less expensive than other options, in part because the wooden pieces may be thinner. The quality of some components also tends to be lower, but you can get around this by upgrading to heavier-duty equipment.

Manufacturers may estimate the time needed for assembly; figure on needing more. The plan, hardware, and lumber for this type of entry-level swing set with a fort and slide will generally cost about $500.

PRECUT PARTS, COMPONENTS, AND A PLAN

Companies that specialize in play sets sell kits with all the necessary parts, including lumber already cut to size, drilled for bolts, smoothed, and stained.

How much time you save over doing the prep work yourself depends on the quality of the kit and which tools you own.

In some kits, the wood is simply cut to length, drilled, and stained. In others, every edge is rounded over and every bolt hole is counter-sunk—jobs that can take a while even with the best of tools. Some factories pre-assemble railings, floor panels, and other sections, which saves you time. Hardware and other components on these play sets may be identical to the parts furnished with kits at

Rainbow Play Systems sells this structure, the Huckleberry Hideout, with all precut pieces ready to be assembled.

lumberyards. Sometimes they can be considerably better.

Stores that specialize in play sets generally encourage customers to pick and choose features they want. These stores may also send a designer to your home to help work out the best configuration for your yard. Plan on spending about $1,500 for a kit that includes precut lumber.

INSTALLED PLAY SET By paying a set installation fee, you can arrange to have a manufactured play set delivered to your home and completely assembled. Fees vary by the company and the complexity of the set, but generally average about $300.

CUSTOM DESIGN

If you build it yourself, a custom play structure doesn't need to cost any more than one of similar size that's assembled from a lumberyard kit. You and your kids get exactly what the family wants. But doing it on your own will probably take longer at every step, from finalizing the plan to buying parts to actually building the structure.

Finding fittings for play-set staples such as swings and slides is no problem. Look at lumberyards, home centers, and specialty play-set dealers. Residential- and commercial-quality parts are also widely available over the Internet.

The other way to get a custom design is to hire someone to create it. Garden shows sometimes feature companies that specialize in this craft. Their designs may be quite imaginative. If you see one you especially like, don't hesitate to ask what it costs. The displays are often for sale.

Deck builders and general contractors can also build custom play sets, but they may want to work from your design. A sketch or a model is often enough to give a builder an idea of what you want.

Custom designs can be built to the same safety standards as manufactured play sets, but it's up to you to make sure. For in-depth information about safety issues regarding specific types of play equipment, consult publications from the U.S. Consumer Product Safety Commission (see Resource Guide).

Prices range from a few hundred dollars to the cost of a small house in a rural community ($100,000 and more).

For some families, a colorful custom structure like this one by designer Barbara Butler is worth the price.

SHOPPING FOR QUALITY

Whether you're eying ready-made play sets or shopping for parts to build one yourself, you'll find a range of options for every component. Here's a checklist of issues to consider.

WOOD

• Is the wood rot-resistant (see page 20) and has it been stained?

• How hefty are the pieces? Minimums are 4-by-4-inch posts, 4-by-6-inch swing beams, and ¾-inch-thick deck boards. For heavy use, go with thicker wood or extra supports.

• Are edges smoothed and corners rounded, especially on railings and platforms?

HARDWARE

• Is the hardware residential or commercial quality? A residential swing hanger must carry 80 pounds (160 pounds on two chains). Commercial ones hold 5,000 pounds.

• What type of steel has been used? "Ductile" steel is more brittle than the steel used in stamped parts. Either will work, but ductile may snap if fasteners are overtightened.

• How many lag bolts are there, and are holes drilled for them? Be aware that some "predrilled" kits have holes only for bolts that need nuts.

• Does metal rub against metal in key spots, such as swing hangers? Hangers with nylon bushings last longer. Bronze bearings lubricated by oil sealed into the fitting are even better.

• Are S hooks, snap hooks, or caribiner clips used to fasten chains or ropes? It's easy to swap swing styles with snap hooks and clips, and they close securely. S hooks are dangerous if they are only partially bent shut.

ROPES AND CHAINS

• How heavy are they, and what load are they designed to carry?

• Is the chain coated? Plastic film reduces the chance of pinched fingers, but the coating cannot be repaired.

• Polyester rope is softer to touch, less stretchy, and more sun resistant than nylon.

• If rope is doubled back on itself to create a loop on the end, how securely is the loop fastened in place?

• Does rope present a safety hazard? There is no risk of strangulation if both ends are fastened and the slack allows only a 5-inch circle to be formed.

STABILITY

• Which age range is specified on manufactured equipment rated for residential use? A set described as suitable for children ages 2 to 5 may tip if older children use it.

• Do metal braces and bolts with nuts (not just lag bolts) fortify key joints, such as those between the swing beam and the play set's legs? Joinery that allows wood to rest on wood is usually quite strong; connections that rely only on nails or screws are weaker.

• Is the structure designed so that legs or braces form triangle shapes? Triangles are more stable than right angles.

FORTS

• How spacious is the fort? Is the space below useable?

• What is the roof type? Wood costs more than a tarp, but lasts longer.

• Are there at least two ways to get up and down? Multiple ways in and out boost play value.

• Do your kids have ideas to accessorize the fort? Creating special features can be as much fun as using them.

SWINGS

• How high is the swing beam? The higher the beam, the more thrilling the ride. But the higher the beam, the larger the area of safety surfacing you need.

• Are swing seats soft and flexible? These are safer than those made of hard materials.

• What is the spacing between swings, and do the ropes or chains angle out above the seat in order to minimize side-to-side movement? The minimum standard for residential sets is 8 inches between swings, but chains may hang straight down.

• Does the play set come with a glider swing? This feature is quickly outgrown and can really hurt a child who gets in the way.

SLIDES

• How much do you want one? Preschoolers love slides, but the attraction often fades around kindergarten age.

• How is the slide constructed? Single-wall slides often need to have 2 by 4s bolted down the sides for stiffening. Double-wall slides are stronger.

A PLAY SET INSTALLER'S TIPS

Most play structures begin as kits of some type that must be assembled. Does it make sense to tackle this job yourself, saving hundreds of dollars? Or should you hire it out? Judge for yourself by seeing how Tony Lerma, a professional installer for Rainbow Play Systems, erected a simple play structure in just 2½ hours.

1 Lerma begins by assembling the fort's leg structures. With a rubber mallet, he pounds a bolt (with washer) through a predrilled hole. He leaves the nut only hand-tightened because he won't adjust the structure to be plumb and square until it is erect.

2 The bottom brace uses lag bolts. Holes for this type of screw are not predrilled—and there are 121 of them. Lerma drives one in with a ½-inch impact wrench in about 1 second. Homeowners using a socket wrench need to predrill every hole and then tighten the screw with a wrench.

3 To erect the legs without a helper, Lerma wraps his own leg around a post to hold it upright while attaching a bottom brace. When both leg assemblies are up, Lerma pushes handfuls of mulch under low spots until his torpedo level shows that the structure is flat.

4 Flooring sections come next. Because they're pre-assembled at the factory, Lerma just bolts them in place. He tightens the nuts after checking to make sure the diagonal distance between opposite corners is equal, a sign that the floor is square, not trapezoidal.

8 Attaching the slide is quick. It takes just two pan head screws, which are wide and flat on the back. If burrs develop, setting the screw head deeper, sanding the hole edge, and adding a dab of silicone caulk fixes them. This slide has stiff double walls, so it doesn't need the wooden stiffeners required with single-wall slides.

9 Building the swing beam support structure is a bit like piecing a jigsaw puzzle together. With a special A-frame brace loosely bolted to the legs and the swing beam, Lerma rests one beam end on the fort and hoists the other end until the legs swing underneath and give support. The structure is complete.

5 With the floor in place, Lerma uses it as a platform to erect the rest of the fort. He adds the remaining beams, then the rails, which also come pre-assembled from the factory. One way pros get the job done fast: They know exactly where every piece goes.

6 Assembling the tarp roof is a snap—literally. Screws with snap heads hold it in place. With the screws snapped on, Lerma drapes the fabric in place and taps with a hammer to mark their locations. Then he snaps off the screws and fastens them to the wood.

7 Lerma attaches the ladder with lag bolts. Depending on whether the ladder goes on the side or the front, he may need an extra piece to ensure a child's head can't be trapped. If the gap between the top rung and the fort's deck exceeds 3½ inches, he blocks it with a board.

combo climber

For kids who love to climb, this play set offers plenty of challenges. It packs in four climbing choices: a spider web and a cargo net on the front and a climbing wall and a vertical challenge on the back. The structure also features a lookout platform, two swings, and space for two sandboxes, one under each of the A-frames. Kids can also use the A-frames as playhouses.

John Dufresne, of Signature Research Inc., a company that creates ropes courses for camps and conference centers, designed this structure to be easy to build with materials that are readily available. The rope and webbing, which may be harder to find, can be purchased from his company (see Resource Guide). They also sell ready-made spider nets.

When building play equipment, be sure to follow these two very important design rules, which will prevent a child's head from becoming stuck in the structure: there should be no openings between 3½ inches and 9 inches, and no downward-pointing parts should form an acute angle less than 55 degrees. In this climber, two clever details keep the rope and webbing from slipping into unsafe shapes. The spider web is made of hollow polyester-Dacron™ rope, which is flexible enough to be spliced or interwoven at each intersection. And the cargo net has a pop rivet wherever its nylon webbing crosses. However, the web and net should still be inspected regularly.

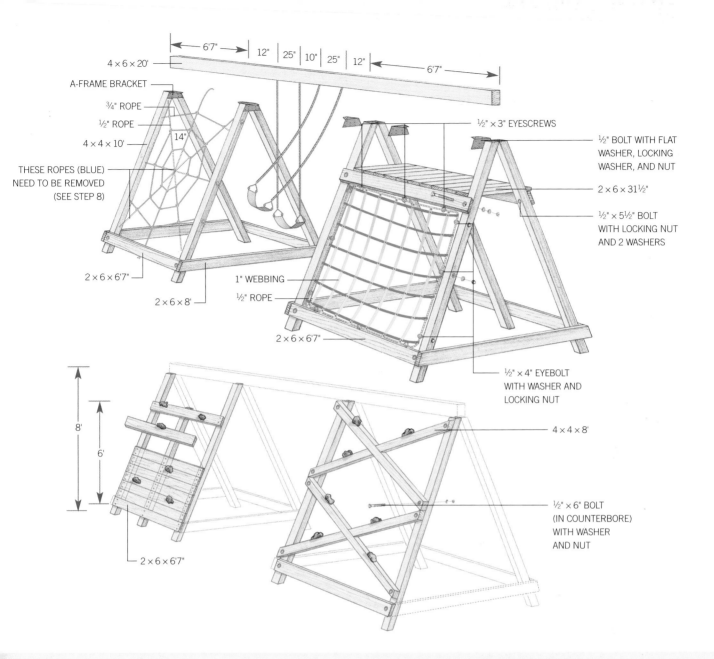

4 × 6 × 20'

6'7" 12" 25" 10" 25" 12" 6'7"

A-FRAME BRACKET

¾" ROPE

½" ROPE

4 × 4 × 10'

14"

THESE ROPES (BLUE)
NEED TO BE REMOVED
(SEE STEP 8)

2 × 6 × 6'7"

2 × 6 × 8'

1" WEBBING

½" ROPE

2 × 6 × 6'7"

½" × 3" EYESCREWS

½" BOLT WITH FLAT
WASHER, LOCKING
WASHER, AND NUT

2 × 6 × 31½"

½" × 5½" BOLT
WITH LOCKING NUT
AND 2 WASHERS

½" × 4" EYEBOLT
WITH WASHER AND
LOCKING NUT

8'

6'

2 × 6 × 6'7"

4 × 4 × 8'

½" × 6" BOLT
(IN COUNTERBORE)
WITH WASHER
AND NUT

MATERIALS

- One 4 × 6 × 20' beam
- Eight 4 × 4 × 10' rot-resistant framing posts
- Five 4 × 4 × 8' rot-resistant climbing supports
- Twenty-four 2 × 6 × 8' rot-resistant planks for bases, platform, and climbing wall
- Six ½" × 4" eyebolts, with washers and nylon locking nuts
- Eight ½" × 6" lag bolts, with washers and locking nuts
- One box 3" galvanized deck screws
- Twenty-two ½" × 5½" bolts, with nylon locking nuts and forty-four washers
- Five ½" × 3" eyescrews

- Eight or twelve additional ½" washers
- Six A-frame brackets (see Resource Guide)
- Twenty-eight climbing holds, with bolts and T nuts
- Seventy-nine feet ½" polyester-Dacron rope (includes ring around cargo net)
- Seventy-eight feet ¾" polyester-Dacron rope
- One hundred feet 1" tubular nylon webbing
- Forty-nine pop rivets, with washers for back
- Two swings with belt seats and mounting hardware
- Masking tape
- Six ½" bolts, with flat washers, locking washers, and nuts (narrow enough to fit through bracket)

BUILDING THE FRAME

1 Metal brackets used on standard swing sets speed the construction of this climbing structure's frame. To determine the slope of the A-frame legs, simply copy the bracket angle, 26 degrees in this case. Trim off a small piece at the top of the 4 by 4s so the wood fits together and matches the shape of the bracket. While the 4-by-6 top beam is still on the ground, screw and bolt it (through the center hole) to the end pairs of legs and gently tip the structure upright. Then slip in the two inner pairs of legs. Screw and bolt them in place.

2 The vertical climber on the back of the structure consists of two big Xs made from half-lapped 4-by-4 posts. To determine the angle of the end cuts and center notches, temporarily screw on one crosspiece, hold the overlapping piece in place, and have a helper mark the intersection and the ends. Then take out the screws, cut the posts, and reinstall them. To cut the notch, use the method shown in step 2 on page 68.

MAKING THE CARGO NET

3 To assemble the cargo net, install a ½-inch rope around the opening on the climbing structure. Thread the rope through eyebolts on the sides and eyescrews on the top. On this climber, instead of splicing the ends at the bottom to create a continuous loop, the builders created an eye splice on one end (see page 117) and tied a Prusik knot, a type of sliding knot that's easily adjusted, on the other. Thread the rope through the eye splice and double it back, leaving about 3 feet of excess. Hold both ropes about 18 inches from the eye, with the free end on the bottom. Bring the free end under and then over the main rope twice in the direction of the eye. Then, without tightening the knot, move the hand that's feeding the rope two or three inches farther from the eye. There, loop the free end over and then under the main rope. Arrange these winds so they go back toward the first part of the knot. Tighten the knot and slide it along. Weave the end of the rope into the part of the end loop that does not slide. If the cargo net becomes slack later on, tighten it by sliding the Prusik knot.

4 The cargo net is made of nylon webbing. Like rope, webbing tends to unravel when cut. Wrap the area to be cut with masking tape, make the cut, then singe with a match or propane torch.

5 To keep the cargo-net openings 11 inches wide, install a pop rivet at each place where the webbing intersects. Use a washer on the back to keep the rivet from pulling loose. Also use pop rivets to hold the net to the play structure. Loop ends of the webbing over the perimeter rope, then install a pop rivet through each overlap.

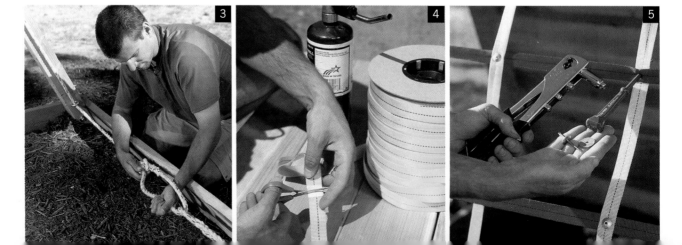

MAKING THE SPIDER NET

6 The spider net consists of two rings and two partial rings made from ¾-inch-thick rope intersected by four spokes of ½-inch rope. From the thicker rope, cut three pieces 104 inches long and one piece 188 inches long. After singeing the ends, create the outer circle from the longest rope and the inner circle from a shorter piece. Using a knotting technique known as a "short splice," form the rope into a circle and temporarily tie the overlap together so that 7½ inches of each end is excess. Untwist one of these tails and tuck the free strands into the twisted rope, one strand at a time. Weave in the opposite direction to the twist in the rope (see page 117). After weaving each strand into the rope three times, weave in the other set of free strands in the opposite direction, also three times. Snug everything as tight and as smooth as possible. Don't let go of the rope until both sets of loose ends have been woven in.

7 Arrange the rings on a flat surface so they are 14 inches apart. Lay the spokes on top so they intersect at the center of the smaller circle. The diagonals are 15 feet long, the vertical is 13 feet long, and the horizontal is 9 feet long; all include excess for knots. At each intersection, thread the ½-inch rope through a twist in the ¾-inch rope. Tie a simple overhand knot to lock in the position.

8 To attach the spider web to the frame, start with the vertical spoke. At the center of the top and bottom framing pieces, drill a counterbore 1¼ inches wide and about ¾ inch deep into the back of the framing. This hole should be large enough to hold a knot and a washer with a ½-inch hole. Continue to bore through the wood with a ⅝-inch bit. Poke the spoke rope through the hole and through a washer. Tie a simple overhand knot on the end, snugging it up tightly to the washer. Tie up the horizontal spoke and install the diagonal spokes at the top of the net. Cut the spokes where they intersect in the center circle and tie them off or weave each one back into itself. Pull the diagonals taut at the bottom.

Depending on the stretch in the rope, you may be able to attach the diagonal to the bottom or side framing piece without creating a space that could trap a child. But if a 9-inch sphere can't pass through easily, leave the diagonals hanging while you knot the partial ring into the side framing pieces 28 inches up from the bottom. Then splice the lower ends of the diagonal ropes back into themselves. At the top of the net, you may choose to attach the partial ring to the sides 83 inches up from the bottom. But if the top opening underneath the diagonal isn't wide enough for a 9-inch sphere to pass through, double the partial ring back into itself. (Illustration shows the ropes doubled back at top and bottom.)

a challenging climbing wall

A well-designed climbing wall packs more fun into a small space than any other playground feature. Unfortunately, some climbing walls are so easy to master that they merely whet children's appetites for climbing. This wall, however, offers a full meal of challenges, enough to get kids from beginner level to skilled climber.

The crucial part of any climbing structure is a series of holes through which ⅜-inch T nuts can be fitted. The nuts' internal threads fit bolts on climbing holds, which are sold at outdoor-supply stores. The bolts and nuts have a thin coating of zinc, which helps to prevent rust. For added rust resistance, smear a bit of grease on the bolts before inserting them into the T nuts.

The wall must be attached to a very sturdy surface. Some play sets provide the needed heft, while others must be beefed up so they can't wobble or lift. Here, the manufacturer suggested adding a series of redwood stakes (2 by 2 by 16½ inches) next to the 2-by-6 bottom beam opposite the climbing wall. Pound the stakes flush with the top of the beam and then screw them to it. Be aware that manufacturers generally void their warranties when owners modify play sets by adding climbing walls or other features. When the wall is tilted open, it creates a gap that could trap a child who tries to climb around to the fort. Canvas closes off the opening.

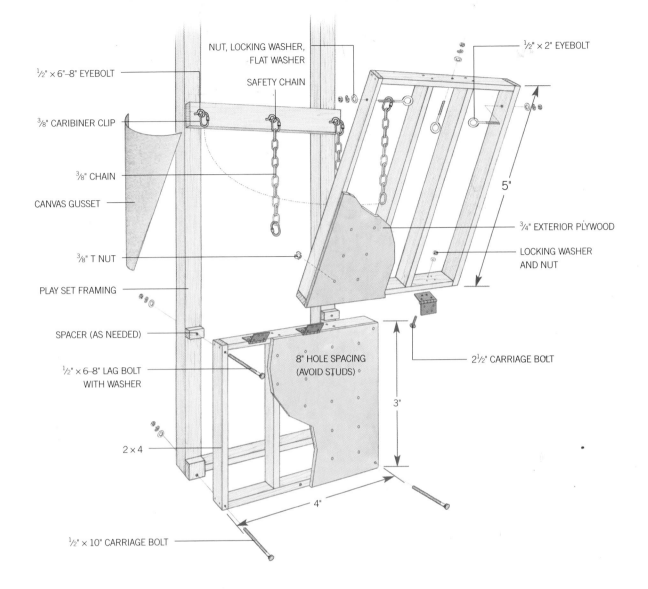

½" × 6"–8" EYEBOLT

NUT, LOCKING WASHER, FLAT WASHER

SAFETY CHAIN

½" × 2" EYEBOLT

⅜" CARIBINER CLIP

⅜" CHAIN

CANVAS GUSSET

⅜" T NUT

PLAY SET FRAMING

SPACER (AS NEEDED)

½" × 6–8" LAG BOLT WITH WASHER

2 × 4

½" × 10" CARRIAGE BOLT

¾" EXTERIOR PLYWOOD

LOCKING WASHER AND NUT

5"

2½" CARRIAGE BOLT

8" HOLE SPACING (AVOID STUDS)

3"

4"

MATERIALS

- Six framing pieces, 2 × 4 × 8'
- One sheet ¾" exterior plywood
- One box 2½" deck screws
- One box 3" deck screws (32 screws needed)
- Three heavy-duty door hinges
- Twelve 2½" carriage bolts, with locking washers and nuts (select bolt width that fits through hinge)
- Sixty ⅜" T nuts
- Three eyebolts, ½" × 6"–8" (long enough to go through play structure framing) with washers and nuts
- Three eyebolts, ½" × 2", with washers and nuts

- Three ⅜" chains, each approximately 2' long
- Six ⅜" caribiner clips
- Three lag bolts, ½" × 6"–8" (long enough to go into play structure framing), with washers
- Two carriage bolts, ½" × 10", with washers and nuts
- Granite spray paint
- Purchased holds, which come with T nuts and hex bolts
- Two canvas gussets, with screws to attach to structure, sized for the wall's maximum tilt
- 1" screws (for canvas)

BUILDING INSTRUCTIONS

To build the wall, measure the space available and make adjustments as needed. This wall is sized to match a single plywood sheet, 4 feet by 8 feet, which was divided into a fixed panel 3 feet high and a tilting panel 5 feet high. Framing consists of 2 by 4s set on edge, spaced so vertical studs have centerlines 16 inches apart. Screw the framing together with 3-inch rust-resistant deck screws.

Drill holes for the T nuts and install them before you fasten the plywood to the framing, using the framing as a work surface if you need one. There is no firm rule about hole spacing. Some climbers like a precisely regular pattern; others mark off a grid but then deviate from it slightly when they drill, to produce holds that are randomly placed.

The tilt mechanism consists of heavy-duty hinges and adjustable chains on both sides of the top part of the wall. A third chain, installed at the maximum length, acts as a safety break in the middle of the wall in case kids try to adjust the side chains themselves.

The length of the chains sets the maximum amount of tilt, so you can choose what's suitable for your situation. Even a few degrees add considerably to the challenge of climbing. Die-hard climbers aim to master a 45-degree angle.

Before mastery, of course, come many attempts that don't always work out right. Be sure to provide adequate safety cushioning under the wall and for 6 feet out from the top edge when the wall is at maximum tilt. If the play structure design allows a child to climb around the edge of the wall, add a piece of canvas screwed to both sides to block the space between the wall and the play structure.

When children begin using the wall, secure it in the vertical position and provide plenty of beefy footholds and easy-to-grip handholds. As the children's skills advance, add challenges by tilting the wall, incorporating skinnier holds, and spacing the holds farther apart.

1 After framing the wall sections, lay out holes so they miss the studs. Spacing holes about 8 inches apart provides maximum flexibility without sacrificing the plywood's strength. Drill with a piece of scrap wood underneath the plywood so holes don't fray.

2 Smear waterproof glue on the outside of the T nuts and hammer them into place from the back. They must go in straight and seat fully so the prongs lock into the wood, preventing the holds from spinning. When all the nuts are in place, turn over the plywood and screw it to the framing with 2½-inch deck screws. Space these screws about 8 inches apart along the studs.

3 Install hinges while the wall panels are still on the ground.

Align hinges so only the barrels project beyond the plywood. For added strength, attach the hinges with bolts that extend through the framing, rather than with wood screws. Use carriage bolts, which have rounded heads.

4 Raise the panels into place and check to make sure the design meshes well with the play structure. Then, while another person steadies the top, screw the lower panel into place. Three lag bolts were used here across the top of the panel and two long carriage bolts hold the bottom edge. To accommodate this play set, a 4-by-6 beam was added at the bottom to keep the wall plumb.

5 Connect the chain to the play structure and to the wall with heavy-duty caribiner clips with a hex adjustment screw that can be tightened with a wrench. Change the wall's tilt from a ladder. Adjust one side, move the ladder, and then work on the other chain.

6 Standard hardware on climbing gear consists of coarse-thread ⅜-inch bolts and T nuts. Because the bolt heads have a hex indentation, you can use a hex wrench to tighten them.

bicycle tricks

In mountain biking circles, a sport known as "North Shore" freeriding is considered one of the most exciting. Devotees ride their bikes through woods laced with obstacles, such as teeter-totters, narrow log bridges, and multi-tiered jumps. In the extreme, it's a sport most parents would prefer their kids admire only from a distance. Toned down, however, it's great backyard fun.

Christian, 15, was hooked after a family visit to a resort that offered freerider trails suitable for cyclists of all skill levels. Freeriding combines the obstacle-course concept of "trials" biking with the jumping and speed incorporated in BMX racing. Back home, Christian set about building routes of his own, mostly with scrap wood. Because rigging up new challenges is half the fun, he doesn't worry about building contraptions that will withstand the elements or last a long time. He builds, masters the trick, and then starts inventing fresh feats to test his skill.

Two years ago, a track flat on the ground seemed challenging. Now, that's something he builds to introduce younger kids, including 8-year-old Sam, to the sport.

BUILDING A TEETER-TOTTER

A teeter-totter for bicycle riders consists of a base topped by a slatted frame that pivots on a ½-inch galvanized bolt threaded through holes in the frame.

The teeter-totter must be designed so that it returns to the starting position on its own. There are two easy options for making this happen. Either make the front section (where the biker enters) a few inches longer than the exit, the solution used here. Or add a weight underneath the entry area.

Although a teeter-totter can serve as a stand-alone place to play, connecting it to other sections of track makes riding more fun. Christian makes all sections the same width and just butts them together when they are on the ground. When he elevates tracks, he screws sections together and to their supports.

Far left: *Having mastered the basics of freeriding, Christian adds new challenges by creating tracks that are higher and skinnier. To make sure the tracks won't slip off his sawhorses, he screws the support pieces to wide boards and then screws those boards to the sawhorses. For an elevated teeter-totter, he adds a diagonal brace at the pivot point and attaches a 1-by-2 vertical guide to the top to make sure the track doesn't slip sideways, off the base.* **Left:** *To allow the teeter-totter to pivot easily, avoid overtightening the nut on the bolt.*

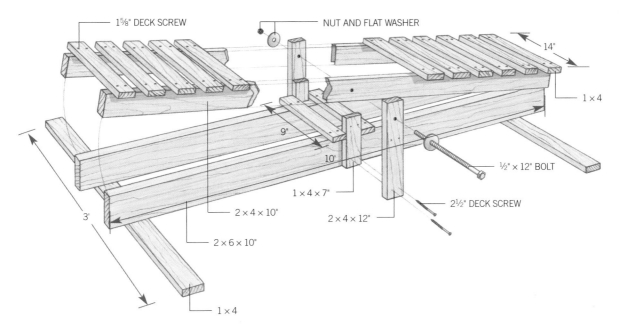

1⅝" DECK SCREW
NUT AND FLAT WASHER
14"
1 × 4
9"
10'
½" × 12" BOLT
1 × 4 × 7"
2½" DECK SCREW
2 × 4 × 10"
2 × 4 × 12"
3'
2 × 6 × 10"
1 × 4

MATERIALS

FOR THE TEETER-TOTTER

- Two supports and uprights, 2 × 4 × 12'
- Two base pieces, 2 × 6 × 10'
- Cross pieces, cut from three 1 × 4 × 10' boards
- One galvanized bolt, ½" × 12", with two ½" flat washers and one nut
- Galvanized deck screws or nails, 1⅝" and 2½"

For each additional track section

- Two base pieces, 2 × 4 × 12'
- Cross pieces cut from three 1 × 4 × 10' boards
- Galvanized deck screws or nails, 1⅝"

FOR THE ROLLER COASTER (page 110)

- Base pieces: two 2 × 8 × 12', two 2 × 8 × 8'
- Cross pieces cut from four 1 × 4 × 8' boards
- Galvanized deck screws or nails, 1⅝"

FOR THE JUMP RAMP (page 111)

- Assorted firewood pieces
- Plywood, ½" (or thicker), one piece approximately 2' × 4', one approximately 2' × 2'
- Two plywood wedges, about 3' long, angled from 6" to 12" wide (or more)
- About a dozen nails or screws
- Dirt

BUILDING A ROLLER COASTER

An easy North Shore–style roller coaster consists of a series of wooden humps topped by wooden slats. For a beginners' course, Christian made the humps about 8 inches higher than the base track and cut the support pieces into a curve about 4 feet wide. He drew the shape freehand and cut it with a reciprocating saw, although a jigsaw or coping saw will also work.

Christian spaced the humps so that the peaks were about 8 feet apart. Sam, trying the ride for the first time, got over the first hump easily, then veered off onto the lawn. With a ride so low to the ground, he had no difficulty remaining upright to the end.

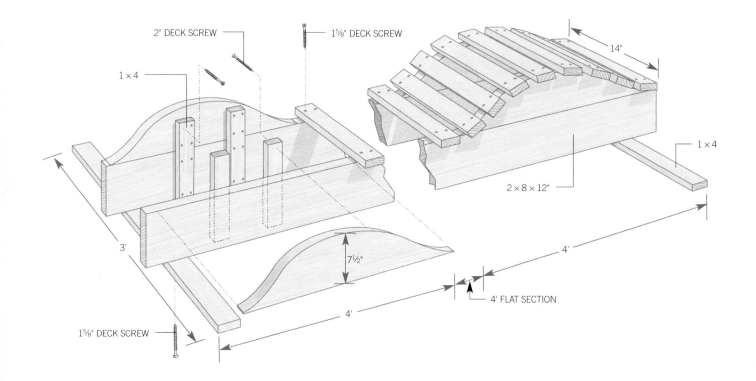

2" DECK SCREW

1⁵⁄₈" DECK SCREW

1 × 4

14"

1 × 4

2 × 8 × 12"

3'

7½"

4'

4'

4' FLAT SECTION

1⁵⁄₈" DECK SCREW

BUILDING A DIRT JUMP RAMP

A jump ramp allows a biker to experience the momentary thrill of becoming airborne. Although he's built ramps of wood, Christian says dirt ramps are easier to build and adjust. A little difference in the curve, especially near the lip, affects how high the rider can get.

To avoid having to shovel too much soil, he stacks firewood as a base. (Hay bales or rocks will also work.) Two big pieces of firewood placed vertically in the middle give good support for the top of the jump. Smaller pieces go horizontally, perpendicular to the direction the rider will travel. Wedge-shaped pieces of plywood screwed to the firewood create the rough shape for the launching-ramp sides. Christian fills in the remaining space with dirt. Packing it in tight, he shapes the top of the pile into a curved lip.

On the back half of the woodpile, Christian lays down a piece of $\frac{1}{2}$-inch plywood as a landing ramp. This ramp is very important because it eases the effect of the landing on the rider's spine. Christian's found that plywood stands up to the force of impact better than dirt. He makes the landing ramp a little lower and a little less steep than the launching ramp.

For beginners, Christian fills in the space between the launching ramp and the landing ramp. As riders become more experienced, they usually want a real gap (and higher ramps).

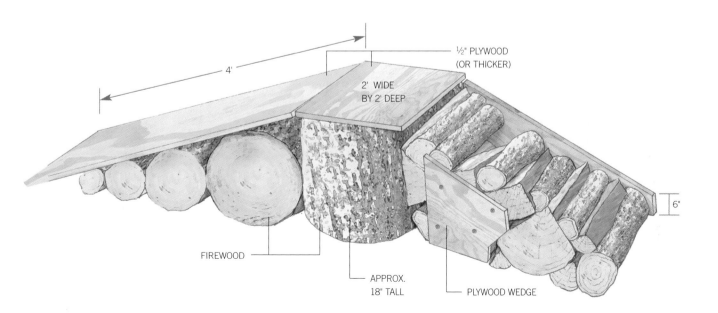

4'

$\frac{1}{2}$" PLYWOOD
(OR THICKER)

2' WIDE
BY 2' DEEP

6"

FIREWOOD

APPROX.
18" TALL

PLYWOOD WEDGE

skateboard ramp

For kids who love to test their physical limits—and have parents with nerves of steel—a ramp takes skateboarding and roller blading to a whole different level.

This ramp was built for a born daredevil. As a three-year-old, Mitch used his plastic play structure as a ladder to the roof of his family's house. By 11, he was eager to hone his skills on a skateboard and roller blades. He pestered his parents for a skate ramp until finally, as a Christmas present, his dad and a carpenter friend built one. With a surface as big as a full sheet of plywood, it's ready at the side of the driveway whenever Mitch or his friends want to let off some steam. The structure is just lightweight enough so that they can pull it out where there's enough room to maneuver. This also allows parents to drag it out of harm's way when no one is around to keep an eye on the action.

The trickiest part of the construction is the first step: establishing a curve that will allow the skater to become airborne. To simplify the process, use a thin piece of wood about 8 feet long as a compass. Extend a 3-inch screw through the piece 2 inches from one end to create a pivot point and, 88 inches past that, drill a hole wide enough for a pencil. Working on a flat lawn or other suitable surface, set out a sheet of $\frac{1}{4}$-inch plywood and poke the pivot screw into the ground at the distances shown in the illustration at right.

Depending on the setup, you may need to have one person apply slight pressure on the pivot screw while another person moves the compass in an arc to trace the curved line on one of the side pieces.

BUILDING INSTRUCTIONS

Cut out the curved piece with a jigsaw. Trace the shape to make two more pieces the same size. Be sure to align all three pieces so the grain of the outside plywood veneers runs in the same direction, in line with the bottom edge of the ramp.

Next, prepare the framing pieces. Cut the wood to make seven pieces $43\frac{1}{2}$ inches long, five $46\frac{1}{2}$ inches long, two 49 inches long, and two 36 inches long. Save the two longest scraps.

Using one of the curved plywood pieces as a template, trace the top part of the curve onto one end of each 36-inch piece and each scrap piece. Cut these curved lines with a jigsaw. Then screw together the back and bottom of the frame as shown in the illustration using 3-inch screws. You will need to cut a notch across one of the wide faces of the crosspiece that goes at the center back. This notch should be $\frac{3}{4}$ inch deep and $\frac{3}{4}$ inch wide so that the notch in the support can slip into it.

Select two of the curved plywood pieces for the sides and attach them to the other framing pieces with lag screws, as shown. Use the remaining plywood piece for the ramp's center support. In this piece, cut a notch $3\frac{1}{2}$ inches wide and $\frac{3}{4}$ inch deep at the center of the back edge. Also cut away the plywood so it will fit around the top and bottom crosspieces at the rear of the ramp.

On the curved edge of this piece of plywood, cut six notches 3½ inches deep and 1½ inches wide. Locate them so that the first notch is 14 inches from the top corner and the others are approximately 7 inches apart. After you cut these notches, use the plywood as a template to mark the locations on the side plywood pieces. This will make it easier to line up the 2 by 4s that support the top of the ramp.

Screw the center plywood support to the framing with 2-inch screws. Slip in the 2 by 4s that will support the top of the ramp and attach them with 2-inch screws. Staple on the ¼-inch plywood, one sheet at a time, leaving the excess in the front.

If necessary, add a few screws to lock the plywood in place. Sink the screw heads just enough so they are flush with the surface.

Painting the ramp or coating it with a pigmented stain will protect the wood against damage from the sun's ultraviolet rays.

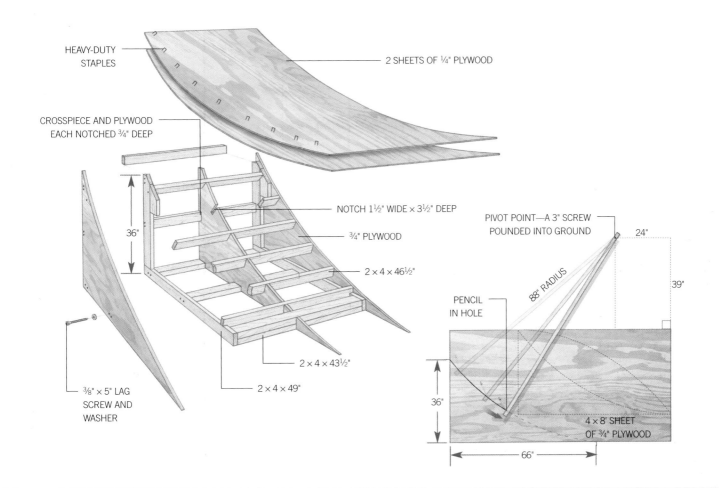

HEAVY-DUTY STAPLES

2 SHEETS OF ¼" PLYWOOD

CROSSPIECE AND PLYWOOD EACH NOTCHED ¾" DEEP

NOTCH 1½" WIDE × 3½" DEEP

¾" PLYWOOD

36"

2 × 4 × 46½"

2 × 4 × 43½"

2 × 4 × 49"

⅜" × 5" LAG SCREW AND WASHER

PIVOT POINT—A 3" SCREW POUNDED INTO GROUND

24"

88" RADIUS

39"

PENCIL IN HOLE

36"

4 × 8' SHEET OF ¾" PLYWOOD

66"

MATERIALS

- Eight 2 x 4 x 8' framing pieces
- One sheet ¾" exterior plywood
- Two sheets ¼" exterior plywood (marine-grade preferred)
- Eighteen ⅜" x 5" lag screws, with washers
- Galvanized or coated screws, 2" and 3"
- Heavy-duty 1" galvanized staples
- Thin piece of wood, about 1 x 2 x 8', to use as compass

tempting tetherball

Fun for beginners yet challenging to those who want to master the sport, a tetherball court makes a great addition to a family play area. Because the ball can't go sailing off, even a single child can have fun batting it back and forth. Two children can stage a rousing game, and bigger groups can play in rounds.

Boys will be boys. Sean, 7, finds a new way to have fun with a tetherball.

Adding to the appeal, tetherball courts are the ultimate in simplicity: just a securely anchored metal pole surrounded by a circular court with a radius as wide as the pole is tall. Players stand on opposite sides and hit the ball in opposing directions, each attempting to get the ball past the other enough times so that the cord becomes tightly wound around the pole.

Although children can play on poles that reach just 7 feet high, 10-foot poles are better as an investment because both children and adults can use them. A solid pole, bought where plumbing supplies are sold, stands up far better than the sectional poles provided with some tetherball kits. To allow 10 feet above ground, the pole needs to be about 12 feet long.

About 4 inches from the top, drill a hole for an eyebolt, using a twist drill. Squirt a little oil on the bit to keep the bit from over-heating. Anchor the pole in a 2-foot-deep cylinder of concrete. A hole diameter of 18 inches works well unless the soil is loose, in which case it should be up to 24 inches.

A pole 10 feet above ground dictates a playing court 20 feet in diameter, plus at least 3 feet of clear space all around. Kids love playing tetherball on lawn, but grass wears thin if the court is used often. Gravel and pavement stand up to heavy wear. Avoid bark mulch, especially types with big pieces, which are hard to play on. Placing the court on a driveway often works well, provided the post is set so that it can be removed when not in use.

CREATING A REMOVABLE POST

With a little extra work, you can anchor a tetherball pole in a way that makes it easy to remove when the court space is needed for other activities. Instead of placing the pole itself into concrete, set a "sleeve" made with a 2-foot length of pipe one size larger than the tetherball pole. Before you add the concrete, slip the pole into the sleeve and place a level against it so that you can make sure the pole is perfectly upright. Tempor-arily tape the gap between the two pipes so no concrete splashes in. Later, whenever you remove the pole, screw a cap onto the sleeve so that it remains free of debris.

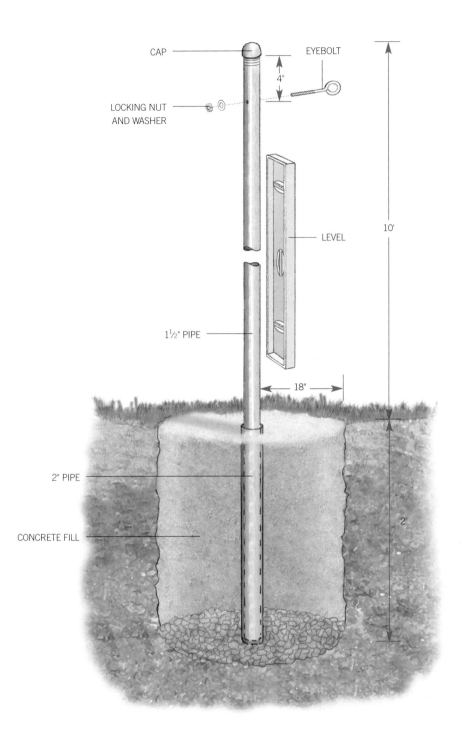

CAP

EYEBOLT

4"

LOCKING NUT
AND WASHER

LEVEL

10'

1½" PIPE

18"

2" PIPE

2'

CONCRETE FILL

MATERIALS

- Galvanized pipe, nominal 1½" × 12', threaded on one end
- Galvanized base pipe, nominal 2" × 2', threaded on one end
- Caps to fit pipes
- Concrete mix, 18 bags (60 pounds each)
- Eyebolt, 2½", with locking nut and washer
- Tetherball on 7' cord

an old-fashioned swing

In playground settings, swing sets definitely qualify as "active play" devices. But at a home, a single swing invites quiet contemplation as well. What better place to lazily drift back and forth than under the arms of an old apple tree?

Although it's possible to rig up a swing by looping rope over a branch, the constant rubbing is likely to wear away the bark and damage the tree. This swing uses a better attachment system: forged eyebolts threaded through the branch. The bolts, which are available from arborists and industrial-supply companies, have continuous metal eyes that can't open up. A washer and a locking nut hold each eyebolt on the back. A tree swing can hang from chain or rope. For rope, the most durable option is polyester, which stretches less than nylon and better resists damage from the sun's ultraviolet rays. Manila hemp, a natural fiber, has a traditional look and feels pleasantly smooth to the touch. Despite the name, it's made from fibers of a plant related to the banana. An inch-thick rope carries a load of 1,215 pounds, which is plenty for a swing.

The owner of this swing ran the rope through holes in a wooden seat for a continuous strand. At each end, she wove a loop, known as an "eye splice" (see illustration at right). Long used by sailors and ranchers, this type of eye is durable and reliable. It's also possible to make a loop by bending back one end of the rope and lashing it in place with wire. Either way, it's a good idea to reinforce the eye by stretching it over a metal thimble.

Check swing equipment frequently, especially when it's rigged from parts not specifically manufactured as play equipment. Manila rope sheds water and is fairly durable outdoors, but it does eventually rot. Eyebolts, caribiner clips, thimbles, and other metal parts that rub may also wear out and need to be replaced periodically.

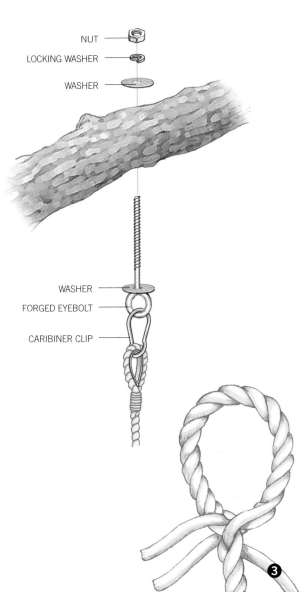

NUT

LOCKING WASHER

WASHER

WASHER

FORGED EYEBOLT

CARIBINER CLIP

1) Tuck this strand under a strand in the rope.

2) Thread this strand under the next strand in the rope.

3) Flip the eye over and tuck the third strand under the only remaining strand in the rope.

4) Complete the eye by repeating the first three steps twice more. Trim ends.

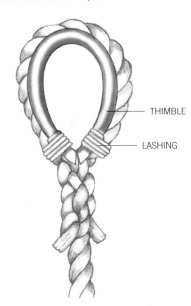

THIMBLE

LASHING

5) Reinforce the eye. Splice with a metal thimble. If the eye does not stay in place, lash it on.

MATERIALS

- Manila rope, 1" thick, twice as long as the swing's reach plus the width of the seat plus 4'
- One piece oak or other wood for seat, 6" × 24"
- Two ³⁄₈" forged eyebolts, long enough to extend through branch, with four ³⁄₈" flat washers and two ³⁄₈" locking washers and nuts

- Two ³⁄₈" caribiner clips
- Two metal thimbles, sized for 1" rope
- Thin wire for lashing thimble to rope

a jiggling balance beam

Very young children enjoy the challenge of the simplest balance beam: a 4-by-4 post laid onto a flat patch of grass, sand, or other play surface. Once they master that, they'll be ready to try this challenging beam, which dangles from chains.

Find a site where there are no sharp obstructions within 6 feet. Begin by digging two holes with center points about 10 feet apart. Place the end posts in the holes, leaving 9 to 12 inches aboveground or above the top of whatever mulch layer you will add. Then backfill, using either sharp-edged gravel (for a temporary installation) or concrete mix (more sturdy). Tamp the fill into place as you go.

Meanwhile, prepare the balance beam. About 8 inches from one end, drill a hole 1¼ inches wide through the beam. With the same bit, drill three holes at each end: one that's 4 inches deep goes in from the end; the other two, counterbores about ½ inch deep, go into opposite sides 4 inches from the end. Switch to a $^{5}/_{16}$ bit and extend the ½-inch-deep holes through the wood. The chains ride in the wide holes and are locked into place by intersecting bolts that fit into the narrower holes.

Drill into the posts for the eyebolts in a similar two-step process so all nuts will be recessed within the wood.

To assemble the balance beam, install an eyebolt in each end post. Thread chain through each end hole and slip a 3-inch hex bolt with washer in through the side. Wiggle things around until the bolt intersects a link. Add a washer and locking nut so that nothing slips. Thread the third piece of chain through the remaining hole in the beam. Cover the chains with tubing to prevent kids from getting their fingers pinched. If you can't find tubing that's wide enough to fit over the chain, get a bicycle tire tube and cut it to fit. Secure all bolts with washers and locking nuts. Then hook the chains to the eyebolts with caribiner clips. Tighten them using an adjustable wrench.

The side posts keep one end of the beam fairly stable, but the other end sways and bounces enough to challenge even an adult. Expect kids to master the entire length before you do—and then to move on to find new things to balance on. Younger kids may also sit on the beam to lazily swing or use it to rock a baby doll to sleep.

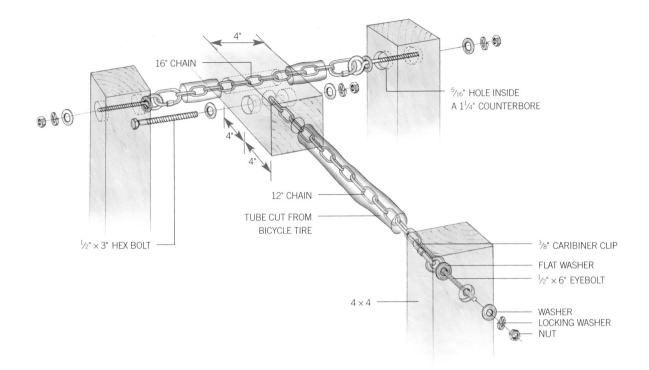

16" CHAIN

4"

$\frac{5}{16}$" HOLE INSIDE
A 1$\frac{1}{4}$" COUNTERBORE

4"

4"

12" CHAIN

TUBE CUT FROM
BICYCLE TIRE

$\frac{1}{2}$" × 3" HEX BOLT

$\frac{3}{8}$" CARIBINER CLIP

FLAT WASHER

$\frac{1}{2}$" × 6" EYEBOLT

WASHER
LOCKING WASHER
NUT

4 × 4

1 After marking the center point of each end of the balance beam, use a 1¼-inch spade bit to drill a 4-inch-deep hole wide enough for the chain to fit with some room to flex.

2 Slip a bolt through the side of the beam to intersect a link of chain and lock it in place. Make sure the holes go through the same face on both ends of the beam.

MATERIALS

- Two posts, 4 × 4 × 6' (each cut to make two 3' pieces)
- One post, 4 × 4 × 8'
- Four eyebolts, ½" × 6"
- Two hex bolts, ½" × 3"
- Six ½" locking washers
- Twelve ½" flat washers

- Four bags concrete mix or gravel
- Four ⅜" caribiner clips
- Chain rated for 1,250 pounds, two 12" long, one 16"
- One bicycle tire

cable ride

If you've never been on a cable ride, chances are you'll grin ear to ear the first time you take one. Riders grip a pulley device, lift up their feet, and zip down a length of aircraft cable before coming to a gentle stop as the cable ascends near its end.

Not every yard can accommodate a cable ride, but, when conditions are suitable, it can be the hit of the neighborhood. The best situation is a level or slightly sloping yard with two sturdy trees at least 40 feet apart to use as end posts. If anchor trees don't exist, it's possible to build artificial supports, but this requires thick, well-braced posts set 4-to-5 feet deep into concrete. Do not attach cables to masonry walls, roof overhangs, or other structures without much strength. The cable route must be clear of obstructions for 6 feet on either side and should be located away from paths or other places where people walk. Metal cable presents a real hazard if passersby hit it with their head or throat.

Plastic trolleys suitable for children's rides up to 70 feet are sold as kits, and heavier-duty metal trolleys, which can go for 150 feet or more, are sold as parts for systems you assemble yourself (see Resource Guide). The kits include instructions for installing the cable so that it has the right amount of slack to provide a fun ride and a safe stopping point. If you buy a trolley separately, you're on your own to design the setup.

The metal cable on which the trolley rides must be attached so that it is slightly higher at the beginning point than at the end, or the ride won't be fun. Dave Carlson of the Outdoor Fun Store (see Resource Guide) recommends a rise of 6 inches per 10 feet. The height should be set so that the tallest riders won't hit their feet on the ground at the lowest point of the ride. A starting point 2½ feet taller than the tallest rider may work, but you will need to test the setup. The amount of slack also makes a difference.

Although kits call for slack and gravity to stop riders at the end, it's a good idea to install a tire bumper. Carlson favors attaching the cable to forged eyebolts inserted through the trees, rather than wrapping the cable around the trunks, as kits specify. Be sure to buy forged eyebolts as standard eyescrews are unsafe. They can pull out, snap, or open.

Cable looped around trees can wear through bark and injure the critical cambium layer below. If you do decide to attach the cable this way, rest the cable in a sling, such as an inside-out bicycle tire. Avoid wrapping cable tightly against a tree because it will force the cable into a sharp bend, which will weaken it. Align cable clamps so the round section lies against the main stretch of the cable. The screw section goes against the short end of the cable.

Cable rides require regular inspection. After every 50 rides or so, check the bolts and tighten them if necessary. Replace any cable that has frayed.

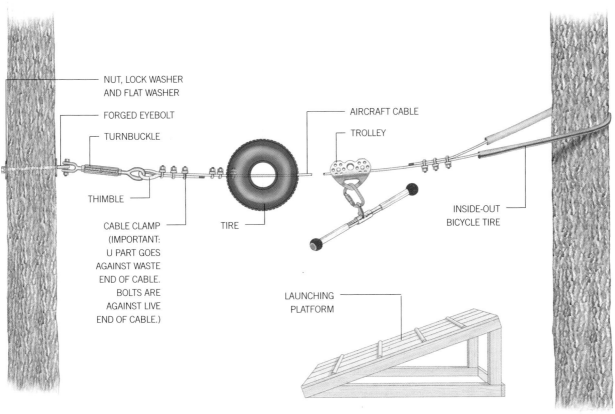

NUT, LOCK WASHER AND FLAT WASHER

FORGED EYEBOLT

TURNBUCKLE

THIMBLE

CABLE CLAMP (IMPORTANT: U PART GOES AGAINST WASTE END OF CABLE. BOLTS ARE AGAINST LIVE END OF CABLE.)

TIRE

AIRCRAFT CABLE

TROLLEY

LAUNCHING PLATFORM

INSIDE-OUT BICYCLE TIRE

PREFERRED ATTACHMENT SYSTEM FOR EACH END

ALTERNATE ATTACHMENT SYSTEM FOR EACH END

CONNECTION AT FAR END

Start with the turnbuckle extended as far open as possible. Grip the cable with pliers and pull until it's as tight as you can make it. Lightly fasten the cable clamps and check tension. You may need to repeat this several times until the cable is taut enough. Then tighten the cable clamps, taking care not to overtighten. Make the final adjustment with the turnbuckle. Check all connections frequently and retighten as needed.

MATERIALS

- Trolley
- Stainless-steel (type 304) aircraft cable: ¼" for rides under 150'; ⅜" for longer runs
- Lawn tractor replacement tire
- Galvanized eye-jaw turnbuckle, ¾" × 18"
- Stainless-steel thimble
- Nine stainless-steel cable clamps

FOR PREFERRED ATTACHMENT SYSTEM

- Two forged ⅝" eyebolts, long enough to go through anchor trees at attachment height with 2" to spare
- Two nuts, two lock washers, and two flat washers to fit bolts

FOR ALTERNATE ATTACHMENT SYSTEM

- Old bicycle tire
- Enough extra cable to loop around trees

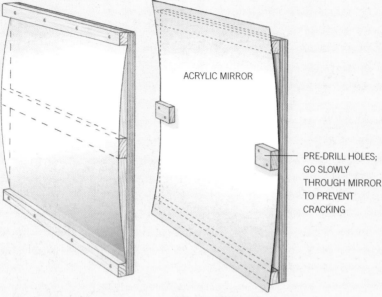

ACRYLIC MIRROR

PRE-DRILL HOLES;
GO SLOWLY
THROUGH MIRROR
TO PREVENT
CRACKING

BEND-OUT MIRROR   **BEND-IN MIRROR**

BOUNCY SWING

When kids tire of swinging back and forth, give them another direction to move: up and down. Add-on swings with a spring mechanism allow children to bounce up and down as they swing back and forth. The spring apparatus can be purchased with either a disk seat or a belt seat. It's designed to fit most play sets that have a swing beam.

FUN-HOUSE MIRROR

Kids love mirrors, and those that make them look taller or shorter or funny-faced just add to the merriment.

Children can make an inexpensive convex mirror from a Mylar™ balloon. Instead of filling it with helium, which might allow wind to carry the mirror away, fill the balloon partly with water and then top it off with air. To get water inside, gently poke a drinking straw down the balloon's throat and let water dribble down the straw. The balloon may need to be repositioned periodically so that kinks in the Mylar don't block the water flow.

When the balloon is partly full, puff through the straw to fill the rest of the space with air. A taut surface reflects best. Remove the straw, and the opening will seal itself. Place the mirror on lawn or soft sand—any non-sharp surface that can get wet if a flood occurs.

For a more official-looking fun-house staple, buy a piece of ⅛-inch acrylic mirror, available at some plastics companies and window shop (see Resources Guide). Plexiglas mirror is also an option, but acrylic works better as a contorted mirror because it is more flexible.

With a piece of plywood backing, wooden spacers, and screws, you can create mirrors that bend in and out like a wave (see illustration above). Or make one that bends out and one that bends in and put them side by side.

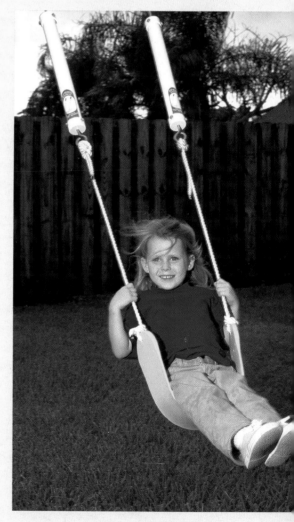

STEERING WHEEL

Play set manufacturers offer plastic steering wheels, which are popular with young children who use them to drive off to fires, into space, and a million other places. Choose one of these plastic wheels, or check out an automobile salvage yard for a real steering wheel.

HAMMOCK SWING

A hammock swing is another option, one especially favored by older children who love to swing gently as they read or chat.

Hammock swings designed specifically to fit swing sets are available. These nets hang from both ends of a horizontal bar that is linked to the swing beam rope and chain.

Standard hammocks are too long to fit into the swing part of most play sets. But the play set can be used to anchor one end. A small support post would be needed for the other end.

TELEPHONE SYSTEM

A length of plastic tubing, two funnels, and two hose clamps are all that children need to create a phone system that allows them to pass messages from one end of a play structure to the other. To keep the tubing from sagging and to prevent accidental strangulation of a child, secure the tubing to the framing of the play structure with pipe clamps.

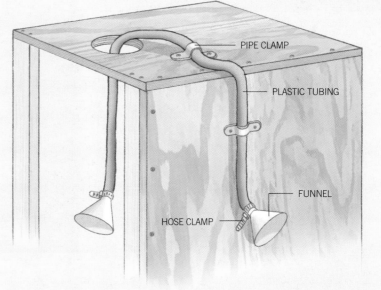

PIPE CLAMP

PLASTIC TUBING

FUNNEL

HOSE CLAMP

PEEPHOLE

For a playhouse or a fort, a peephole or secret window can be great fun. Depending on how the structure is built, this feature may work best in a door or a wall. Choose a place that will be easy to cut and fun for the kids (see Stockade Fort, pages 72–75).

Drill a hole wide enough for a jigsaw or coping saw blade. Then slip the blade into the hole and cut out the rest of the opening. Heart-shaped peepholes are easiest to make by drilling two big holes, perhaps with a blade designed for doorknob holes. Finish making the heart shape by cutting the rest of the wood away with a saw.

From plywood or a scrap of wood, cut a flap large enough to cover the hole. Leave enough extra wood on the top of the flap so that you can fasten it loosely to the wall above. Insert a washer as a spacer before you screw the flap into place so that the little door can pivot open. Add a handle near the lower edge of the flap, if desired.

BARREL ROLL

A plastic barrel, available at home improvement stores, makes a great ride-on toy, especially in yards with a gentle slope. Set on end, it becomes a beefy pillar for construction projects.

LIP BOARDS

Kids make good use of pieces of plywood or boards that are long and sturdy enough to turn into ramps and platforms. For maximum safety and usability, screw cleats near the ends so that the boards have a lip that can be slipped over boxes, ladder rungs, or other parts of play equipment. The lip adds stability and helps to keep pieces from slipping.

CLEAT

photographer credits

Teena Albert/Barbara Butler Design: 22 B
Bill Bachmann/Photo Network: 6 L, 20
Robert J. Bennett: 17, 25 B
Courtesy of Barbara Butler: 96
Claire Curran: 100, 102 all, 103 all
Chad Ehlers/Photo Network: 45 T
Scott Fitzgerrell: 18 BL, 21 TL, 21 TM
Frank Gaglione: 1, 5 TR, 5 BR, 6 R, 19 BR, 26 BR, 28, 30 TL, 30 all, 31 TL, 31 TM, 31 TR, 31 MR, 31 BR, 34, 36 all, 37 all, 42 all, 43 all, 60, 62 all, 63 all, 72, 74 all, 75 all, 88 TR, 104, 106 all, 107 all, 118, 119 all, 124 L
Jerry Harpur: 27 T
Alex Hayden: 98 all, 99 all
Saxon Holt: 11 (D)
Katie Howlett: 25 T
Jeanne Huber: 124 R
Courtesy of Katelyn's Kastles: 49 L, 49 M, 49 R, 88 B
Chuck Kuhn: 5 TL, 5 BL, 32, 33 all, 40, 41 all, 50, 52, 54 all, 55 all, 56, 58 all, 59 all, 66, 68 all, 69 all, 70 all, 71 all, 76, 79 all, 80 all, 81 all, 82 all, 83 all, 84 all, 85 all, 88 TL, 98 all, 99 all, 108, 109 all, 110, 111
Courtesy of La Petite Maison Playhouses: 45 BR
Bruce Leighty: 91, 123 R
Charles Mann: 11 (A), 11 (B), 11 (C), 11 (E), 11 (G)
James M. Mejuto: 22 T
Gary Parker: 64
Jerry Pavia: 11 (F), 11 (H)
Courtesy of Practical Folly Playhouses: 45 BM
Courtesy of Rainbow Play Systems: 95, 123 TL
Courtesy of Sierra Hills Stone: 89 R
Courtesy of Spring Swings: 122 R
Courtesy of Star Lumber: 45 BL
Thomas J. Story: 4, 7 B, 16, 18 all but BL, 19 all but BR, 21 TML, 21 TMR, 21 TR, 21 B, 24, 26 TR, 26 BL, 27 BL, 27 BR, 31 BL, 38, 39, 44, 47 L, 47 R, 90, 112, 125 all
Courtesy of Swing & Slide: 94
Christopher Vendetta: 20 B, 120
Linda Quartzman Younker: 2 all, 3 all, 7 T, 8 all, 9 all, 10 all, 12, 13 all, 14 all, 15 all, 86, 114 all, 116

acknowledgements

We would like to thank the children and families who contributed their time, design ideas, and building skills to the projects in this book. Special thanks to David and Kaza Ansley; John, Krista, and Eric Seeley; Alison Cheung; Candace and Erik Jagel, Sean, Lucas, and Liam; Andrea, Brian, Katie, and Ian Mackin; Lisa Cardus, Rick LaFrance, Malia, and Joseph; Denise, Bryan, Garret, and Autumn Johnson; Kirk Bradley; Jill Slater; Nancy, Bill, Matt, Chris, and Graham Baran-Mickle; Jacob Shore; Elizabeth, Max, and Lucky Welch; Joyce Ansley, Robin Capwell, and Sophia Ansley-Capwell; Neil, Tina, and Mitchell Newman; Dana, Bart, and Christian Berg; Jeff Powers, Debby Haase, Ken, and Charlie; Amy Gonzalez and Isabella Daniel; Jim, Tais, and Michael Barbera; Cynthia, Julie, and Bryan Del Fava; Emily Yeates; Jeff and Ethan Farro; Chrissie and Miranda Grady; Janie and Rachel Farn; Evan Beemer; Max and Avery Schnelke; Audrey, Greg, and Anne Mak; Janet See and Sam; Vasken, Mary, John, and Anna Guiragossian; Larry Zulch and family; John Dufresne; Adam Bondeson; Robert "Ariel" Stone; Thomas C. Wentz; Loretta A. Musser Brown, Joey Musser, Joy and Bubba Brown; Casey Quiroz; Salvador Robles; Beau Cleary; Tony Pitts; Dane Hartman; Kevin Clarke; and Reed Metcalf.

There were also a number of builders and professionals who contributed to this book. We'd like to thank Jay Beckwith of Beckwith Associates, Forestville, CA; Julie M. Johnson, University of Washington Center for Environment, Education, and Design Studies, Seattle; landscape designer Topher Delaney, San Francisco; Stan Jones, University of Oregon, Eugene; garden writer Peg Tillery, Kitsap County, Washington; landscape architect Susan Goltsman, Moore Iacofano Goltsman, Berkeley, California; Valley Nursery, Tharco ccorrugated products, Algona, WA; Jake Jacob, Anna Daeuble, Bubba Smith and Daryl McDonald of TreeHouse Workshop, Seattle; builder Bob Stanton; Ethan Skylar, Skylar Construction Co., Bainbridge Island; Euginia Woerz and Tony Lerma at Rainbow Play Systems; Joel Carver at Backyard Adventures; Jennifer Goodrich at Swing-N-Slide; George Lamage at Kompan; Bob Gaynor at Spring Swings and More; Roland Radtke at Northwest Recreation; Bryan Gordon and Jose Modan of B. Gordon Builders, CA; and Randy at Katelyn's Kastles.

resource guide

PAGES 8-15

"A Child's Garden: Enchanting Outdoor Spaces for Children and Parents," by Molly Dannenmaier; Simon & Schuster; 1998

"Creating a Family Garden: Magical Outdoor Spaces for All Ages," by Bunny Guinness; Abbeville Press Publishers, 1996

PAGES 12-13

Patricia Strehlow Landscape Design
19230 Forest Park Dr. NE, E216
Seattle, WA 98155
206-417-9551

Sharyn Sowell shadow paper cutting
14922 Valley View Drive
Mount Vernon, WA 98273
360-424-5846
www.sharynsowell.com

Metal Fountain:
Schaefer Industries
PO Box 283
North Lakewood, WA 98259
360-659-2559

PAGE 14-15
Sure Shot basketball goal system
1-888-713-5488
www.sure-shot.com

PAGES 18-19
Dyno-Mites safety glasses, manufactured by Sellstrom Manufacturing, Palatine, IL.
Supplier:
Enviro-Safety Products
516 E. Modoc Ave.
Visalia, CA 93292
800-637-6606
www.envirosafetyproducts.com

PAGES 20-21
Redwood, red cedar and various types of preservative-treated lumber are widely available at lumberyards. One juniper source equipped to ship nationwide (but perhaps not economical for small orders):
Environmental Home Center
1724 Fourth Ave. South
Seattle, WA 98134
800-281-9785
www.environmentalhomecenter.com

PAGES 22-23
Safety Guidelines on Play Equipment:
"Handbook for Public Playground Safety" from the Consumer Product Safety Commission, download free at www.cpsc.gov

Measurements of children at different ages can be found on the AnthroKids database at the National Institute of Standards and Technology,
ovrt.nist.gov/projects/anthrokids/

Barbara Butler—Builder and Artist
325 South Maple St. No. 37
South San Francisco, CA 94080
415-864-6840
www.barbarabutler.com

PAGE 26
Colored Play Sand:
Happy Hues, manufactured by ChromaSand LLC
P.O. Box 31883
Independence, OH 44131-0883
216-901-6530
www.happyhues.com

Silica-free Sand:
KNXX Safe Sand Co.
3371 21st Street No. One
San Francisco, CA 94110
415-820-1481
www.SafeSand.com

PAGE 27
Millstone Fountains:
StoneForest
213 S. St. Francis Dr.
Santa Fe, NM 87501
888-682-2987
www.stoneforest.com

Push-button Self-closing Lavatory Faucet:
Pasco Specialty & Mfg. Inc.
7175 Oakland Mills Road, Building J
Columbia, MD 21046
410-290-8100
www.pascospecialty.com

Float Valve:
Trough-O-Matic Automatic Float Valve (aluminum)
Miller Manufacturing Company
2600 Eaganwoods Drive, Suite 460
Eagan, MN 55121
651-365-3400
www.miller-littlegiant.com

PAGES 32-33
Foam-lined Hose:
Flexogen 6-ply, ⅝-inch hose, manufactured by Gilmour Group, 800-458-0107
Supplier:
Lee Valley Tools Ltd.
814 Proctor Ave.

Ogdensburg, NY 13669-2205
800-871-8158
www.leevalley.com

Self-closing Shower Valve:
Chicago Specialties #350
Manufactured by
Dearborn Brass/ 21st Century
P.O. Box 1020
Tyler, Texas 75710-1020
800-527-8443
www.dearbornbrass.com

PAGES 42-43
"Make Your Own Dinosaur Out of Chicken Bones," by Chris McGowan; HarperCollins, May 1997

PAGE 45
Child-size Accessories for Playhouses:
Montessori Services
11 West Barham Ave.
Santa Rosa, CA 95407
877-975-3003
www.montessoriservices.com

Precut cedar storage shed, available at Home Depot; manufactured by:
Star Lumber
7203 112th NE
Arlington, WA 98223
360-658-6191

Practical Folly Playhouses
3039 Bowen Road
Stevensville, ON
Canada L0S 1S0
866-262-4040
www.practicalfolly.com

La Petite Maison
877-404-1184
www.lapetitemaison.com

PAGE 49
Used Building Materials Association
1702 Walnut St.
Boulder CO 80302
303-440-0703
www.ubma.org

Katelyn's Kastles, LLC
PO Box 11155
Arlington, VA 22210-2155
703-524-3025
www.katelynskastles.com

PAGES 52-55
"Cardboard Carpentry," by Jerry DeBruin, and "Further Adventures of Cardboard Carpentry," by George Cope and Phyllis Morrison.

Supplier:
Learning Things Inc.
PO Box 1112
Olean, NY 14760
800-284-5688
www.learningthings.com

PAGES 64-65
Iron-on Adhesive:
HeatnBond, manufactured by:
Therm O Web
770 Glenn Ave.
Wheeling, IL 60090
847-520-5200
www.theromweb.com

PAGES 66-71
Basement Water-channel Liner:
System Platon membrane
www.systemplaton.com
Supplier:
Perma Dry Waterproofing Services Inc.
608 SW 12th Street
Renton, WA 98055
425-277-1990
For sources in other areas, contact the
North American importer:
Armtec Ltd.
33 Centennial Road
Orangeville, Ontario L9W 1R1
800-265-7622, ext. 223

PAGES 76-83
TreeHouse Workshop Inc.
303 N.W. 43rd
Seattle, WA 98107
206-784-2112
www.treehouseworkshop.com

Heavy-duty Exterior "Star Drive"
Construction Screws:
Screw Products Inc.
223 SW 160th St
Seattle, WA 98166
206-242-8880
www.screw-products.com

Malleable Iron (or Round) Washers:
Tacoma Screw Products Inc.
2001 Center St.
Tacoma, WA 98409
800-562-8192

PAGES 88-89
Signs Made of Recycled Materials:
Katelyn's Kastles, LLC
(see opposite page for contact information)

Soapstone:
For information on possible deposits of
soapstone (also known as steatite) in your
area, check with your state's geology depart-

ment or a local rock and mineral club. See
www.rochhounds.com for a list of clubs.
Many clubs sponsor collecting trips. If you
search on your own, ask permission of the
property owner, forest ranger or other
appropriate official.

Sierra Hills Stone
P.O. Box 572
Angels Camp, CA 95222
www.sierrahillsstone.com

PAGES 94-97
Titan model, three-deck version with
turbo tube slide, manufactured by:
Swing-N-Slide
800-888-1232
www.swing-n-slide.com

Huckleberry Hideout model,
manufactured by:
Rainbow Play Systems
800-RAINBOW
www.rainbowplay.com

"Wendy's House"
Barbara Butler—Builder and Artist
(see opposite page for contact information)

PAGES 98-99
Rainbow Play Systems
(see above)

PAGES 100-103
Signature Research Inc.,
PO Box 26046
Fresno, CA 93729-6046

Bracket for A-frame structure:
EZ Frame Bracket, NE 4467-1
Available at home centers and lumberyards,
made by Swing-N-Slide (see above)

PAGES 104-107
For more details on building climbing walls,
see "Home Climbing Gyms: How to Build
and Use," by Randy Leavitt; Elk Mountain
Press, 1998.

Climbing Holds:
REI Inc.
Sumner, WA 98352-0001
800-426-4840
www.rei.com

Play Set by:
Backyard Adventures
14201 Interstate 27
Amarillo, TX 79119
806-622-1220
800-345-1491
www.backyardadventures.com

PAGES 108-111
More Information about "North Shore"
Freeriding:
www.nsmb.com
604-833-6796

PAGES 112-113
Plans for Other Styles of Skateboard
Ramps:
"Thrasher Presents How to Build
Skateboard Ramps," edited by Kevin
Thatcher; High Speed Productions, 2001.

PAGES 114-115
Tetherball Rules and Equipment:
Regent Sports Corp.
P.O. Box 11357
45 Ranick Rd., Hauppauge, NY 11788
www.regent-halex.com

PAGES 116-117
Manilla Rope:
Lehman's
One Lehman Circle
P.O. Box 321
Kidron, OH 44636
888-438-5346
www.lehmans.com

PAGES 120-121
Heavy-duty Trolley and Installation Parts:
Outdoor Fun Store
3766 Commerce Court
Wayne, MI 48184-2803
734-728-2200
www.outdoorfunstore.com

Lighter-weight Trolley:
Fun Ride Delux, made by:
Spring Swings Inc.
2000 Avenue P, Suite 13
Riviera Beach, FL 33404
561) 845-6966
www.springswings.com

PAGES 122-124
Acrylic Mirror:
Laird Plastics
1400 Centrepark, Suite 500
West Palm Beach, FL 33401
800-610-1016
www.lairdplastics.com

Bouncy Swing:
Spring Swings Inc.
(see above)

Hammock Swing:
Rainbow Play Systems
(see above)

index

Page numbers in **boldface** refer to photographs